THE NEW BABEL

*By the same author
from Triangle/SPCK:*

Rural Rites
Country Matters

THE NEW BABEL

PETER MULLEN

First published in Great Britain 1987
SPCK
Holy Trinity Church
Marylebone Road
London NW1 4DU

ACKNOWLEDGEMENTS

Thanks are due to Faber and Faber Ltd and Harcourt Brace Jovanovich Inc.
for permission to quote from 'The Waste Land' in
Collected Poems 1909–1962 by T. S. Eliot,
copyright 1936 by Harcourt Brace Jovanovich, Inc.;
copyright © 1963, 1964 by T. S. Eliot.

British Library Cataloguing in Publication Data

Mullen, Peter
    The new Babel.
    1. Sociology, Christian
    I. Title
    261   BV625

    ISBN 0-281-04256-X

Typeset by Rowland Phototypesetting Limited
Bury St Edmunds, Suffolk
Printed in Great Britain by
Hazell, Watson & Viney Limited
Member of the BPCC Group
Aylesbury, Bucks

Contents

Preface   vii

1   Babel in the Church   1

2   Babel in the Secular City   17

3   Faith in the Age of Technology   38

4   Stories that Save us   56

5   The New Sectarianism and the End of the World   80

6   The Language of God   96

What are the roots that clutch, what branches grow
Out of this stony rubbish?

      .   .   .

I think we are in rats' alley
Where the dead men lost their bones.

                    T. S. Eliot, *The Waste Land*

Preface

I believe that contemporary society is best described as a
New Babel. We live in a world overtaken by trivialities, by
the exaltation of all that is instant, noisy and unsustaining.
Millions are in thrall to the mass media and thereby to the
advertising men who control it. We have lost touch with
the enlivening power of our cultural tradition. There are
no roots that clutch.

So it is no wonder that we lose faith, that bishops and
synods sound incomprehensible, that prayer seems invalid.
For religion and faith can only be mediated by a living
culture.

In *The New Babel* I have tried to make accurate criticism
of contemporary life and also to suggest a way in which
our cultural life can be restored, our communality recreated and our faith rekindled.

Peter Mullen
February 1986

I

Babel in the Church

The fragmentation of secular society has been mirrored in the decline of the Church. I speak first of the Church of England but similar events have taken place in the Roman Catholic Church and among the Nonconformist denominations. In a word, the Church is no longer the Church, but only a sect – one more club among society's infinite number of clubs and pressure groups. Moreover, the status of sect has not befallen the Church like some awful misfortune; it has been willed upon it by those in places of ecclesiastical authority. Before discussing the nature of this new and extreme sectarianism, I should like to describe what has been lost.

The Church of England was born out of a clash of religious feelings and political animosities so severe that the nation hardly survived. Our impression of the English Church is of such tranquillity and sedateness – 'Stands the church clock at ten to three, and is there honey still for tea?' – that we are in danger of forgetting the violence and volatility which surrounded its origin in the sixteenth century and which continued sporadically for more than a hundred years. When we consider the acrimony, the vested interests of power politics, the martyrdoms and burnings, wholesale laying waste of churches and monasteries, heresy hunts, show trials and regicide, we may think it a miracle that any institution survived, let alone one which has done more than any other to give a kind of unity and sense of tolerance to this nation.

The famous Anglican Settlement made every English man, woman and child a member of the Church of England with rites of passage – baptism, matrimony and a decent burial. Hooker said that all men – even those who we should now say belonged to other denominations – were to be welcomed at Anglican services so long as they came 'meekly, reverently and of a good will'. The vision and compass of this Church was inclusive. It was a master stroke in terms of political achievement and it saved the nation from being torn apart. But there is no cause to idealize the results of this settlement and to imagine a country in which all the people were possessed of a quiet and conforming zeal, working cheerfully on the farm all week then packing the nave on Sunday. It was not so. There have always been keen Christians, enthusiasts for the faith, diligent in practice. But there have always been, also, great numbers of the indifferent, the lapsed and the curmudgeonly, and this fact is acknowledged by the Prayer Book which refers to them as 'the careless' who are to be 'roused'. 'Good' and 'bad' Christians, 'faithful' and 'un- faithful' alike were all considered to be members of the Church of England. This was not a piece of hypocrisy, as if to claim religious affection for those who would not claim it for themselves; it was a work of political genius which gave a visible unity to the nation. Visible in the form of all the parish churches up and down the land and powerfully reinforced by the King James Bible and the Book of Common Prayer, called by Jeremy Taylor 'a treasure house of rare devotion'. It was a workable system, a genuine settlement, which was refined and improved over the following centuries by various Acts for the toleration of dissent – especially those of 1828 and 1829.

The great danger to political stability is enthusiasm, and the Church has suffered shocks of this from time to time: the Methodist schism in the eighteenth century and the Evangelical revival a little later. But these movements were as nothing compared with the manic salesmanship prac- tised by the clergy of today. When noticeboards behind iron railings and under lychgates adopt the slogans and methods of the consumer society, then we must expect the Church to succumb to the same fragmentation as the secular world. 'We Want U in Our Church' and, as I saw by an ancient parish church in Whitby, 'Jesus Now Glorified'. We know the cultural antecedents of that phrase right enough: 'New Improved Daz'. The clergyman and his Parochial Church Council have become salespersons for religion and their job-specification is 'to get people in'. 'Mission', 'evangelism' and 'outreach' are the vogue words along with, of course, 'renewal'. Communications from diocesan offices urge the Church to be 'relevant to today's society' and 'outward-looking'. These communications are often called 'action packs', 'mission modules', 'units' and so on. They are exact replicas of the spuriousness which litters secular society. As in the 'education industry' where the teacher is no longer the character of central importance, so in the Church there are the copies of all those advisers, co-ordinators and resource-persons to tell the parson how to be 'effective' and 'successful'. The 'Clerical Situations' columns in *The Church Times* advertise for experienced parish clergy to move into these posts, to become Directors of Councils for Mission and Evangelism, Advisers on Youth Committees, Secretaries for the Synod's Board for Social Responsibility which issues its reports and minutes and guidelines and recommendations from its various working parties, study groups and teams of specialists. Church bureaucracy is a quango alongside quangos, operating a pressure group among pressure groups competing for a slice of everyone's time and attention.

'Committed' is an interesting word applied indiscriminately to lunatics and to these new sorts of first-class Christians. As I write, the General Synod has just set up a working party to decide whether ways cannot be found of ascertaining the degree of 'commitment' to the Christian faith of couples asking for marriage. Hooker would turn in his grave. Those rites of passage, including matrimony, are available for all English people as and when they are needed. They act as landmarks. Well, the neglected Commination Service in the Prayer Book has a word: 'Cursed is he that removeth his neighbour's landmark.' And all the people shall say Amen.

The new enthusiasts and sectarians who control the Church – the heirs of those whom Cranmer derogated as 'such men who have always discovered a greater regard to their own private fancies and interests than to that duty they owe to the public' – constantly pour forth pamphlets and booklets which purport to give the Church's view on every subject from glue-sniffing to the bomb. This is called 'being socially conscious' and 'relevant'. What is striking is the absence among these church politicians of any reasonable doubt concerning the validity of their moral opinions, their 'private fancies' as Cranmer said. They are confident that they speak 'the Church's mind'. Well, the Church's mind expressed in these booklets full of line drawings and underlinings turns out not to be such as might be derived from St Paul or the Fathers of antiquity but only veneered likenesses of secular utilitarianism. If this is what the mind of the Church is like, why should we take any notice of it? We can, after all, find these opinions rather more carefully expressed in the literature of the moderate wing of the Labour Party and the SDP.

The quality of the advice – usually called the 'recommendations' – is so poor. There is, after all, a limit to the moral elevation that can be delivered surrounded by cartoons of the Holy Spirit as a dove taking a nosedive behind what resembles an open copy of the *Daily Telegraph*. It does not help when these pamphleteers buttress their authority with regular claims that their outpourings are examples of the 'new paths in which the Spirit is leading us'. New paths. New Improved Daz again. Only they are not new, but only what the vacuous consensus has been saying for years. It amounts to bourgeois niceness and the taboo on upsetting people – even the Russians. When the Synod pronounced on the bomb they elected for 'no first use' but no abandonment of the nuclear deterrent. That is to say, tell them we have a bomb but we won't use it.

There is the same unwillingness to offend against the sexual mores of the age. A recent booklet, *Foreword to Marriage* – note the selfconscious aping of the *Guardian*'s chief sub – issued by the Board for Social Responsibility speaks of the honeymoon as 'the closest coming together'. I cannot help thinking that Cranmer would have avoided that *double entendre*. It goes on 'For some couples this will be a new experience on both sides. For others, either husband or wife will already have had sexual experience. For some there will have been full and free experimentation for some time.' It sounds like Mr Heath's old speeches on the Common Market. Roll up, roll up, says the General Synod, rakes, lechers, maiden aunts, old maids of both sexes, both he who hath had it and she who hath not – marriage is for you!

But this is marriage without the commanding moral ideal. Where there is no ideal there is no criterion. And where there is no criterion, we do not know what we *mean* – so how can we know what we *do*? If 'marriage' is a word for all sorts and conditions of relationships, free experimentations and fornication (by any other name, of course) then 'marriage' does not mean anything any more so far as the C. of E. (Revised) is concerned. But no one should expect consistency from the Board for Social Responsibility, not even in its own invented canons of sexual permissiveness. When *Foreword to Marriage* is only an unmusical version of 'Anything Goes', why should the Synod suddenly wax so altogether squeamish about divorce and the second chance? Surely such events can be put down to experience, to all kinds of full and free experimentation – and then forgotten? But no. Suddenly the swinging C. of E.

gathers up its petticoats and ascribes to itself the so recently relinquished habit of moral seriousness. It wants to know of couples desiring remarriage – either one of them having been previously divorced – if they have 'a sense of sin' about their past. Such uncouth language to come from the Board of Social Responsibility after all its fashionable freethinking and latitudinarianism! A sense of sin? It is a bit late in the day.

But the moral and doctrinal malaise goes deeper than the foolish remarks which fill official reports. The continuing decline of the Church is both symbolized and guaranteed by the new liturgy in the Alternative Service Book. I am not going to make here a comparison between the 'beautiful language' of the BCP and the limp prose of the ASB. I have done that already in many places and often. I will confine myself to saying what ought in any case to be obvious: that sacred texts are made what they are by time and use and that to throw out a volume whose phraseology echoes, even at this late stage, throughout common speech is to ask for trouble. Rather I want to point to some of the doctrinal changes which the new book has made – changes which amount to a loss of nerve and a loss of faith, the Church once again trying to be nice, trying not to offend against the euphemistic blandness of the consumer society. Leave the Eucharist on one side for a moment; perhaps it is only for the committed. But look at what has happened to the occasional offices, the rites of passage in which the Church meets the everyday world.

The Solemnization of Matrimony has become 'Marriage Services' – the parson on his feet again, advertising, providing a service for the consumers. This new cleaned-up product does not any longer mention 'sin', 'men's carnal lusts and appetites' or 'fornication'. No offence must be given to the customers: it is a golden rule in salesmanship. We must not seem to be judgemental. But what if the rites of passage mark *crises*? All is euphemistically suffused in the costless happy glow of the bourgeoisie praying to its kindly God. The BCP introduction used to say: '. . . which holy estate Christ adorned and beautified with his presence and first miracle that he wrought at Cana of Galilee.' In the ASB, gone is the 'holy', gone the adorning and beautifying and, of course, gone is the miracle and we are simply told that Christ was himself a guest at a wedding. Not even *the* guest, mind you. Was there ever a clearer case of wine into water? And if all those words about fornication and 'a remedy against sin' are omitted, we are compelled to think that the Church no longer believes those doctrines to be true. What else *should* we believe? What else can we believe, in the absence of occult perception, except what is said by the words on the page? The new Marriage Service is not about any of the things which concerned the Solemnization of Matrimony. The awful spiritual and moral insistence of the old service has evaporated with the omission of those words. How could we have expected it to remain? The attenuated, vacillating, forsworn alternative is epitomized in the form of the new vows. I shall not dwell on this but I must make one more quotation which seems to me to indicate with utter finality the emptiness of the new service. The Prayer Book has the man say, 'With this ring I thee wed'. Six words of one syllable which go back as far as Chaucer and the couple making their promises at the church gate. Were these words amended because we could not *understand* them? In their place we are given: 'I give you this ring as a sign of our marriage'. This is a discarnation. Eleven words of abstraction which fail to do the work of six because, if he has to tell her the ring is a sign, it means *the sign is not working*. Imagine a sign in front of another sign on the motorway: 'This is a sign'. And we always knew the ring was a sign of marriage. When the new book makes us say 'as a sign' it really means 'as a lecture on symbolism'.

And so we come not to the Burial of the Dead but . . .

Funeral Services, from which the inescapable conclusion is drawn that the Church is officially terrified by the dissolution of the body and has no confidence in the resurrection. Liturgiologists who have so little time for corporeality where it is animated – as we hope it is in matrimony – will have even less to do with it when it is deceased. Take, for instance, that confident utterance which the parson used to make, coming down the aisle, preceding the coffin: 'I know that my Redeemer liveth'. This is not in the ASB. But it is a word of faith made more faithful by the music of Handel, words and a tune known by almost everyone. Surely it is the business of liturgiologists to fasten upon and use perceptions like this which go so deep? It is, after all, these modern liturgists who aim to be 'relevant'. They ought, at least, to show some acquaintance with the dialect of the tribe. Why leave out that phrase? The answer soon becomes obvious. Those words are followed by: 'though after my skin worms destroy this body', and a book which will not mention 'fornication' and 'carnal lusts' will hardly bring itself to a remembrance of worms. Ordinary Yorkshire folk learned to have more courage from the later verses of 'On Ilkla Moor Baht 'At'. And the forfeiting of that line about worms means that the next line of immeasureable encouragement has to be given up, too: '*Yet in my flesh shall I see God*'. The loss of nerve led not just to a change of language – messing about with 'mere words' – but to a loss of faith.

There is more discarnation in the nicked and cut version of Paul's Corinthian letter: in the original, in answer to the question of how the dead are raised, Paul says 'Thou fool'; in the polite, euphemistical alternative he only says, 'These questions do not make sense' – as if he were a logical positivist lecturer in philosophy aping Freddie Ayer. This Paul will not say 'corruptible' either, but only 'perishable', which takes us back to the supermarket again for a new pair of rubber boots to replace those that have perished through having been left too near the radiator. 'Earth to earth, ashes to ashes, dust to dust' – 'may in suitable cases be omitted'! 'Vile body' is left out, of course. The BCP mentioned our 'vile body' so that the next line could affirm hopefully 'that it may be like his glorious body'. Leave out the 'vile' and – Ichabod – the 'glory' also departs. Because there is no death in the ASB funeral, there is no assurance of resurrection either. How could there be?

Much of the sales talk of the contemporary Church is about the 'joy' which is to be experienced in worship. Erstwhile evangelists and charismatic revivers make a big noise about the gospel which is of the forgiveness of sins, the wonderful pardon freely given by Almighty God. But this is only good news if we are made to feel the true enormity of our transgressions, the sheer wickedness of evil. Only then could deliverance mean anything worth having. Alas, this is just what the ASB does not allow. All that talk in Cranmer's confessions about the remembrance of our sins being grievous unto us and the burden intolerable is omitted. We do not err and stray like lost sheep any longer. And we know why not: because modern man as imagined by the liturgical revisers does not take kindly to being likened to a sheep. So no such likening will be made. Which only means that the connection between the ASB and the Bible – 'All we like sheep', and the parable of the lost sheep – is severed. Or are we to suppose plans have been laid to 'update' those parts of Scripture, too? It is regarded as morbid and, worse, as 'negative' to dwell on sin. But unless we 'acknowledge' our sins, unless we 'bewail' them – 'our manifold sins and wickedness' – then they will only break out in all kinds of neuroses and other sorts of spiritually paralysing afflictions. Jesus and Paul taught us that lesson. And so did Sigmund Freud. Is the age of Belsen, napalm, mass-starvation and the bomb supposed to be less sinful than Cranmer's?

What is the use of all the salestalk, the glossy leaflets, the affected moral seriousness, the earnest guitar playing and the semi-abandoned dancing in the aisles if there is no underlying reality? Why should anyone bother to join a Church which pretends to have such unusual good news if that news turns out to be only a pale reflection of what everybody in polite society believes anyhow? No sin to speak of. No corpses. No incarnation of intention into solid language. No miracle. No glory. Why all the fuss? A Church which dares not speak to us of earthly things cannot be trusted to speak to us of what is heavenly.

And yet the leading churchmen continue to perform their frantic salesmanship, as if they held in their hands the pearl of great price when all they actually possess are a few beads of paste. How can we put any value on the 'socially responsible' pronouncements which exude from the General Synod when that Synod has spent years in the production and dissemination of a set of church services which have an inadequate sense of corporeality and sin? That lack of understanding means that they do not have a true picture of the nature of man. So how dare they presume to *advise* man? What they preach in fact is a sort of pelagian self-reliance, sanctimonious injunctions to do what the gospel says we cannot do. Because there is no doctrine of sin among these false prophets, there is no doctrine of grace either. Take out those realities and what is left of the gospel except self-satisfaction, hot air and bluff? We must, they say, solve problems that have remained intractable for centuries: abolish poverty and war, make all races and creeds live in harmony and do away with injustice worldwide. It is the ethics of *Blue Peter* and the other 'children's magazine programmes' on television. It assumes we are all jolly nice and that the only impediment to our working these wonders is a dash of unpelagian idleness. Have they never read St Paul and his brilliant statement of the flaw that lies deep: 'The thing I would, that I do not; that which I would not, that I do'?

Where there is no vision the people perish. The contemporary Church evokes no vision of God, of the Presence which disturbs and yet comforts, which is ever-present like a holy haunting at the bounds of sense, the Presence evoked by Moses and the prophets; by the Gospel writers and by Donne and Dante, T. S. Eliot and J. S. Bach. How can preaching which has it all wrong about the nature of man hope to convey something of the reality of God? What sort of God is he who is alleged to inspire the outpourings of the Board for Social Responsibility and to inhabit the syntactical spaces among the announcements of page numbers at an ASB Eucharist? 'Foolish', as St Gregory said 'to look for God beneath the highest creations of man; and impious to put Him there'. But Gregory had not the advantage of the ASB and the Synod's latest pamphlet on multinational companies. We cannot expect a Church with these misapprehensions to provide a spirituality for the waste land. In a desert we need landmarks. Unfortunately, church policy has removed them all.

There is a faction in the Church which imagines it has lifted itself above the miasma of contemporary bureaucracy: the so-called charismatic revival. Devotees claim to be Spirit-filled, to have rediscovered the reality of God, joy in worship and the lost vocation to heal the sick and to cast out demons. The style of worship is unusual. I went to an evening Eucharist at a charismatic church in York. It was full long before the start and the congregation included many young people, students from the colleges and the university, teenagers from the suburbs and commuter villages round about. Banners advertising the Holy Spirit hung from the medieval pillars and a stage had been erected in the chancel. A bearded clergyman came in and greeted the people with a grin. Then he began a series of announcements which were designed to amuse: 'Will anyone look after a big dog, please, that belongs to Jim and Stella?' Jim and Stella stood up and beamed proudly at the rest of the congregation – just as if they had been identified as part of a studio audience. The congregation sniggered. The clergyman smiled a chat show host's smile, finished his shaggy dog stories and announced the first hymn.

It soon turned out that this bearded parson had been only the warmer-up. Another came on and preached a fundamentalist sermon that might have been entitled 'The Good News of Our Damnation', lurid, unbelievable. What happened after this was even more unbelievable and scarcely less lurid. A large, ecstatic lady in the next seat gripped my hand and at once people all over the church left their pews and began to wander about the place. There was a long interlude of chattering, kissing and cuddling, back-slapping and raucous laughter. This part of the service is, of course, called 'The Peace'. It was followed by the mild hysteria which the revivalists call 'speaking in tongues'. It was a peace which passed my understanding.

This sort of worship is highly regarded by many in authority and at least half a dozen bishops are themselves practitioners. They see it as a sign of 'a great new out-pouring of the Spirit'. The bright-eyed youngsters, the enthusiasm, the pop-cosy atmosphere, the twang of the liturgical guitar – it all convinces them there is life in the old Church yet. But the quality of this life is only that of the pop-concert, a mock-ecclesiastical version of tele-vision's audience participation, so-called 'family entertain-ment'. There is work to be done on that word 'family'; there is an exclusive, sinister side to its cosiness. What have these in common: 'family butcher', 'family service', 'family pub lunch' and Charles Manson's sect 'the family'? It has become customary to refer to the congregation as a family; and is the parson the father? At another charismatic church I went to, the vicar, having just returned from two weeks' holiday, began the service by standing on the chancel step and calling out, in passable imitation of the game show host Mr Bruce Forsyth, 'Nice to see you!' Then he bent forward, cupped his hand to his ear and waited for the response, 'To see you – nice!' Yes, it is all very *nice*. That gesture exactly sums up the ambience of charismatic worship: *Game for a Laugh* transposed to the sanctuary.

Well, a bit of pop might be fun at times; even Wittgenstein used to go and watch Hollywood musicals. But let us not imagine we can live on it, as if it were the real thing. At its best it is vacuous, mediocre, empty-headed; and it makes me wonder why, if the Holy Spirit is really behind the new style in religion, it is all so third rate – the same maudlin guitar chords, the pretentious liturgical dancing, the outbreaks of programmed spontaneity, the anti-intellectual sermons in which we are asked to believe what is merely preposterous and to call it piety. Is that what we are supposed to recognize as new life? But we know what life is like and which things display it: organ music by such as Bach, Buxtehude and Olivier Messiaen; the startling prose of the King James Bible and the rhythms of Cranmer's collects; plainchant; the hymns of Cowper and Wesley – 'O thou who camest from above The pure celestial fire to impart . . .' But there is no fire at St Knees Up, only a frothiness which, however, does not refresh the spirit. If only for the style and content of its worship, charismatic revivalism would be a bad thing: for, since it is the form of worship most 'accessible' to youngsters brought up on pop, television and thoughtlessness, it makes the appreciation of genuine forms of worship impossible. The purpose of such as Bach and the AV in worship is not merely an aesthetic one; it is to tell us the truth about God. This truth is not conveyed by unimaginative and repetitive choruses, arm-waving and a mildly libidinous sense of togetherness. The parallel with the effects of television is striking: just as the constant parade across the screen of what is mediocre, undemanding and unnourishing actually spoils our taste for what has real quality and life, so religion as selective fundamentalism and the games show/chat show nexus obscures and finally obliterates what alone can sustain.

But there are even greater confusions in the charismatic revival arising out of the much repeated assertion that 'It is always God's normal will to heal'. Why are so many not healed then? Why have some, in my own parish, died in torment of mind after having been told that God was healing their sickness – one man with a fatal liver disease? What are all these bright young things from the well-to-do suburbs doing, peopling the world with the demons of New Testament times while taking care to obtain science 'A' levels so that they can begin university careers in biochemistry and pharmacology – psychology, even? There is a legitimate language of possession and demon-ology but it belongs in its own cultural epoch. It is not available to us to amalgamate cultural fragments, to speak contradictory languages. Our understanding of the experi-ence which created the language of demons and regular divine intervention must become creative and imaginative enough to produce a coherent description of the same experience in terms of our own culture. The charismatics' teaching on healing and exorcism is incoherent because it fails to explain our actual experience in which people are rarely healed by the laying on of hands and in which alleged manifestations of demons are more usually exhi-bitions of coercive power unbridled in the charismatic housegroup. Here are two sentences which, I believe, offer rival interpretations of a problem which frequently occurs in charismatic groups: (1) 'Jim and Sandra should split up; Satan is in their relationship.' (2) 'Jim and Sandra should split up; I'm jealous.'

The traditional Church is fast disappearing between the devil of charismatic revival and the deep blue sea of bureaucratic ink. It is drowned in the sanctimonious flood emanating from committees and spokesmen, boards and councils who are no longer in touch with the fullness of faith to be found in the English Bible and the English Prayer Book. It is emasculated by strident sectarianism and by the uncritical adoption of techniques and strategies which every day can be seen failing in the secular world. The trend is to ever greater superficiality in the world and in the Church. Even the popular music of a generation ago sounded as if it had not severed all connection with a tradition that included 'folk' and 'classic'. The 'new' thing permanently pursued by those who jam the air waves with their noisy spuriousness must always be simpler and 'more accessible' – which is to say, more banal – than what went before. So the capacity to appreciate any degree of subtlety, nuance or quality is always deteriorating. Even the weekly comics of my boyhood look like literature compared with the almost wordless gaudy tracts that appear on news-stands these days – all filled with references to television. The Church, as a sect in society, is simply doing its best to keep up with the general run of things. That ASB came out in 1980. The Liturgical Commission once said that we shall need a new book – an Alternative Alternative? – by 1990. The real English Prayer Book lasted four hundred years. At this rate we shall produce ASB3 in 1994. 'Tumid apathy with no concentration. Men and bits of paper.'

Perhaps we feel that *something* must be done. The problem is how to proceed, on what basis to begin a restoration when in secular society millions do not know the difference between the objects to be found in station kiosks, ghosted for pop stars and actresses, and a *book*; when we are so far gone into liturgical vandalism that there are half a dozen English versions of the Lord's Prayer. In this climate it is not a question of what to teach but of *how*. Everything visible and invisible is made subject to the new instantaneous jargonizing and sloganizing of the mass media. Our tragedy is that the real and deep concerns of humanity and human feeling simply *cannot* be expressed in those terms: they lack depth, subtlety, thought, reticence . . . silence.

Perhaps spirituality in the new babel has only one method left to it, and I shall try to say something about that in another chapter. It is, in the interim, disturbing to note that in the old chronology there was first Babel . . . and then the Flood.

2

Babel in the Secular City

Western culture is no longer a coherent whole, and society is far gone into dissociation. Provocations and alarms require the support of real evidence: in this chapter I shall try to provide the evidence for my belief that in today's world spirituality, where it is possible at all, is generally futile or sick.

Society is dominated by the mass media and mainly by radio and television. This is to say that men and women define themselves, create their self-image and their view of others, in terms dictated by what appears on the television screen. Children do this too. So the rot starts early. I spend a lot of time with schoolchildren and they tell me what they watch. These are so-called 'children's programmes': Saturday mornings supply three hours of whirling captions, sub-conversational grunts and bad music which are chiefly aimed at producing life-long addiction to the most gaudy materialistic satisfactions. These programmes – *Swap Shop*, *Superstore*, *Saturday Starship*, *Number 73* and the like – are presented by people whose existence is defined by the title 'television personality', a most revealing phrase. For a 'television personality' is anyone who appears regularly on television, the mode or quality of his appearance or the measure of his skill, the standard of his artistry, being entirely beside the point. He, though it can be she, is 'a professional', 'a host', 'an anchorman' who must sit at the blue or pink desk with its telephones and its TV monitor and try to provide the semblance of linkage to the bewildering assortment of items which happen on the screen in three-minute 'slots' all morning. There is a liturgical code governing the appearance and behaviour of the professional anchorperson. Jeans and T-shirt usually. Bright colours always. A tie may be worn if it is loud enough. Uniform unisex. Professionals entirely inter- changeable. Accent non-specific but 'upbeat'. The smile continuous. Switch from one channel to another and they are all the same. No individuality. You do not need personality to be a Television Personality.

The first task of the anchorperson is to maintain any children present – 'the studio audience' – in a state of loud and vacuous excitement. It helps if the children can be given T-shirts with the name of the programme on them – so that they can imagine they too are Television Person- alities. The children in the studio or at home on the living-room carpet are then introduced to children's pro- grammes' English style. Yeh. Right. Right. That's right. They are educated in the knowledge that conversations should be about some piece of expensive trivia that you want to get or to swap; that the most vital area of discourse is that which concerns what was on television last night or what is coming on tonight; that the most important people in the world are pop stars. There is a complete lack of any depth or seriousness among the 'input' which must be kept 'light'. The children are encouraged to 'respond' by shout- ing and cheering when the off-screen production assistant holds up the clapperboard. There is much flashing light and shiny black leather. Pop-stars turn up as studio guests to be interviewed by the Television Personality about their latest 'video' which the children can then watch on the 'studio monitor'. The video is always 'great' or 'amazingly successful' – like the pop star's American tour which was 'fantastic'. No stray word of criticism must intrude. Then it is time for the 'phone-in' when viewers ring to say what they have to swap or what they thought of Kate Kakon's latest video. Sometimes music is played during the solemn display of the 'Top Ten Swaps'; once this was the Sanctus from the *Missa Luba*, a genuine African Mass. On occasions, those phoning-in are asked for, and supply, intimate details about themselves such as the name of their favourite television programme or whether they would like to be part of a studio audience.

Those who produce this cathode Bedlam will say that I am being sour – but they would say 'dead miserable you are'; they will claim (some might think, against all the evidence) that it is 'only a bit of fun'. But even fun must pause for breath, have light and shade. Whatever happened to the contrast button? The language – including the 'graphics' and the 'image', the 'captions', the 'intro', the 'format' – creates the world. The medium is the message. And the message is subhuman, dehumanizing. It is also always the same. Totalitarianism though never so bland. Because it is continuous and there is no alternative it becomes the language of aesthetics by which children judge everything else. But it is the language of the lowest common denominator. To think that out of such as this are constructed the children's standards of criticism! It is no use saying that the children like what they are being given. Reith said, 'Give the people what they like and they will begin to like what they are getting.' That was said in criticism of some of the more trivial aspects of light entertainment in the 1940s. What would Reith say if he could see us now? Of course children will take to what is frothy and undemanding, to what neither inculcates nor requires any standards of critical awareness, to what asks for no powers of attention or concentration, to what fosters the delusion that the world of sense is a grotto in Woolworths – the Superstore. And of course children, no less than adults, are always eager to take in what needs no effort of assimilation. But to build lives on this goo! To imagine it can sustain human beings! It will not do to say that it is not meant to sustain, instruct or educate, that there are other places and occasions for that. For the mindlessness of children's programmes is so pervasive, and notoriously we all take the way of least resistance, of what requires no effort. Minds which are systematically fed on this stuff will not take readily, or even at all, to the substances which can really nourish them. What chance has the junior schoolteacher when the model of expectation for children in groups is the behaviour of the studio audience, and when conversation and music are ubiquitously and most professionally put across as the gabble and grunts of our popular children's programmes?

There is nothing light about this Light Entertainment. It is relentless tedium. The need to keep that smile on full beam. The obsessive search for something 'new' to fill the 'slot'. And when it is found, it is the same as what we had last week, what we shall get next week. The fashion is lurid anonymity. The 'surprise guests' are unsurprising. Where everything is 'special' nothing is special. Human values cannot be expressed in this form, formlessness. Is that what 'format' means – formlessness? 'Shape without form. Gesture without motion.' Nothing between the desire and the spasm.

There are regular attempts to express value, charity – the vogue word is 'compassion'. Homes for dogs. Dogs for the blind. Food for the starving. But charity must have real emotional, spiritual roots. Presented in terms of the format, sandwiched between one piece of inconsequentiality and the next, it is bound to appear as sentimentality, maudlin second-hand emotion. For charity, too, needs to be *learned*. That means it must be taught. And the chiefest of virtues cannot be expressed by banalities. Those programmes are the deprivation of discernment. They replace education of the feelings by the perpetual cheerless smile. How can anyone who puts value on the trinkets and trivia of Superstore be expected to appreciate the value of a human life, the life of one starving in a distant continent? Not by being shown pictures, ever so beautiful pictures, of the starving millions; because the iconographic power of the picture to convince and excite has been subverted by the banal and meaningless pictures that are shown for the rest of the time. We cannot feel real sympathy for the stricken when their images are 'slotted' between Kate Kakon's video and the next 'studio game' where the prize for the winner is a computer game. We only wince at the disjunction. As I heard recently on Radio Two: 'Three pensioners were killed in a house fire in Bradford; now here's Barry Manilow . . .'

It was the Church which used to provide points of reference for everyman from the cradle to the grave. The rites of passage and the seasons and festivals gave significance, a name, to each individual. Now this function is performed by television. To be seen on television is by itself sufficient to confer fame on a person, no matter what he was doing at the time. Bliss to be picked out in a football crowd; to be 'screened' doing ' a street interview' is very heaven. There are folk in my parish who will not come out for Evensong at 6.30 but who gladly stayed up until after midnight in order to see an Epilogue programme I once did for television. They want 'video weddings' these days so that they may glow in the greater light of the small screen brighter than ever they burned by the altar where they were merely in the flesh. To be screened is like baptism. It confers identity. As the girl says in Anthony Burgess's dystopian novel *1985*, 'You was on the telly'. The final accolade.

So what? Does it matter which institution confers identity? Yes, because the nature and quality of the institution becomes, by association, transferred to the individual. The Church stood for Bible and sacraments, for rites which remained valid despite the shortcomings of individual priests. Television stands for an obsession with banality and mindless trivia, a commitment to produce it hour after hour every day of the week, Sundays not excepted. 'You was on the telly.' Do you want to be identified with *that*?

Children initiated into the cult of Superstore grow up

into confirmed adherents to the complete ceremonies of 'chat show', 'game show' and 'soap opera'. The chat show incestuously macabre: the 'Television Personality chat show host' talking about appearing on television to other Personalities who have appeared and who, by definition, are again appearing on television. The game show stuffed full of manufactured excitement: young marrieds demeaning themselves, being gratuitously insulted by the over-friendly question-master, as they lust after prizes in the form of the moth-eaten treasures of this world; ogled and encouraged by those who lust vicariously in the studio audience. The soap opera, all gloss and cliché; imitation real life in which the characters live out the prescriptions of the advertising industry. All rich pickings and cheap sex. Sex as consumer durable, as a parody of human tenderness – people with responses that are 'scheduled'. A card index of stock phrases. A pretence at character and feeling. These miserable forms invade and infect the rest of television's output so that serious subjects are belittled too. They showed a film *The Day After* which was intended as 'a thought-provoking film-documentary about the horrors of nuclear war'. The horrors for me were the characters playing the parts. Who cares if the inhabitants of *Dallas* get their come-uppance courtesy of five megatons or fifty? The issue with which the film pretended to deal – the survival of humanity, to be or not to be? – was settled before the first bomb went off: there was no humanity to be extinguished; those characters were dead already. The 'viewer' is depraved and corrupted by the film because it asks him to feel and express 'care' and 'concern', 'sorrow', 'remorse', 'anxiety' and 'hope' in its own banal terms. And that is to devalue all those big words and the human emotions denoted by them. Corruption and depravity follow because cliché is pornography. To present as human what is not human is blasphemy against the human spirit.

These clichéd images are persuasive. We take them from

the same screen as that which delivers news of the real world. Banality becomes homogenous. The news itself is news-as-entertainment. It has to be delivered to us in a form that requires no attempt at concentration. First the newscaster – the most numinous and highly paid of the Television Personalities – fashionable, glamorous. She tells what she is about to tell us. Five-second fragments of news so that we are not overtaxed by demands on our attention. Then the captions roll. Then another newscaster tells us what is to come later in the programme. Then, when we imagine we are about to hear the news read, we get 'But first . . .' and there is talk about another 'item'. So the news itself is trivialized by being told backwards, forwards, over and again, upside down in between the whirling captions and a few bars repeated of brash unrepeatable music. There is no time for the intensity of events to sink in. This morning's rail crash, beautifully filmed in the snowy cutting among the pine trees, is down the programme by evening, sandwiched between a heart-lung transplant and a pop-star's divorce. The fast procession of items paralyses any human, emotional response. We cannot respond humanly to such a plethora of events in twenty-five minutes, no, not even when care is taken to end on a 'humorous' note. So the events of the day, worldwide, become 'packaged' between muzak and smirks as well as between, say, *Game for a Laugh* and *Dynasty*. Are we supposed to care for a world so carelessly treated by the television producers?

Television and radio are the universal mode of looking and listening; everything comes to be seen in their terms. In the beginning, there seemed to be some almost religious awareness on the part of those who worked in broadcasting of the awful responsibility which had descended upon them. Should newsreaders be seen? Should they even be named? Real life is holy. Tones must be reverential, subdued. Nowadays they dance on the holy ground of human experience in thigh-length boots to the music of a pop-

group. The result is of human experience demeaned. The
holy ground is desecrated.

Television and radio compel us into passivity. We become 'viewers', 'listeners' and because broadcasting is
commercial, 'consumers'. And as daily life becomes mod-
elled ever more closely on the pattern discerned on the
small screen, our ordinary dealings are shaped in accord-
ance with that televisualized passive consumerism. We
expect service – 'Are you being served?' – from professionals. Human bonds are replaced by formalized encounters
with professionals and experts. The family doctor becomes
the general practitioner. His practice is conducted from a
'centre' and consists largely in dispensing the appropriate
drug. A typical experience: old Harry's wife died 'on the
stroke of the ten o'clock news' as he said – television is the
measure even of our passing from life to death. By the time
I arrived on the scene, Harry was at his next door neighbour's house, with a cup of tea and a cigarette. Enter the
GP, rushed, tired, overworked. He released the body to the
care of the ambulance men and the hospital mortuary.
Then he turned to Harry and offered him the green tablets.
'Take these, and if you have a drop of whisky or rum in the
house wash them down with that.' Harry looked puzzled.
'It's all right,' said the doctor, 'they are precipitated
by alcohol'. Harry looked more puzzled. I could see he
was struggling with 'precipitated' and perhaps a half-
remembered earlier usage of it, sixty years before at school,
'precipitation in the Amazon rain forest'. 'Go on,' the
doctor spoke reassuringly, 'they're quite safe. They're for
mild anxiety'. So that's what we have when our partner for
fifty years dies, is it, mild anxiety! What must happen
before we get severe anxiety? The doctor meant to be kind
but kindness, gentleness and human sympathy cannot be
conveyed by the language of the professional and his
system. It is what Carlyle, Dickens and Lawrence warned
us against: society as mechanism, the abolition of feeling.

And the deprivation of feeling makes any life of the spirit impossible. The emblem of the age is the tranquillizer.

It is Orwell's nightmare come true and our language gives us away. In the jargon of the social services 'in care' really means that someone is being institutionalized because others *do not care*. And 'caring agencies', 'medical institutions' and the like, those very areas of social life which were designed to be palpable expressions of good will, create ill will. Jean, for instance, was rushed off to the psychiatric hospital one afternoon as an emergency. The children had been getting her down and, as a neighbour explained to me, 'She just seemed to crack up, all of a sudden like'. When I went in to see Jean, she was in a public room the size of a tennis court. At one end of this room a group of teenage patients sat apathetically around a loud-speaker which was playing aggressive pop music at top volume. They hardly seemed to be listening. At the other end of the room, a few sad old ladies sat under a television set fixed high on the wall and broadcasting *The World This Weekend* at the same volume as the pop music. Jean sat exactly half way between these rival bedlams, glum, tranquillized, unheeding. No one was attending her. I could not avoid the thought that, if she were not mentally ill already, she soon would be. The 'method' of dealing with her 'case' was all anti-human, lacking in tenderness, the very last thing needed by a person who was profoundly ill at ease. To return to the Orwellian metaphor: there is no need for torture by rats and Room 101 when we have valium and Enlightened Mental Health Care.

If tenderness is all but abolished in human life, it is altogether absent from circumstances of human death. Two examples. First, Harry's wife's disposal at the municipal crematorium. The place all sham-antique wood panels, but on one side a triple-glazed window behind which lurked an artificial garden so sumptuous it would have made Balder sneeze. The coffin wheeled in on a trolley that looked as if it belonged in the supermarket. The service conducted in a piping, thin voice by a nervous curate who seemed more concerned with the need to press the right button on the lectern than to say a word of human comfort to old Harry. A button to make the coffin lunge forward at the end. A button to draw the curtains. A button to summon up funereal muzak – it was Harry Secombe with some schmaltzy ballad. It made me think of a black comedy by Joe Orton. The gadgets got in the way of pity and grief, anaesthetized them, made everyone edgy, wondering whether something might go wrong, worried about how to *be* a grieving relative in that dehumanized citadel. As George Eliot said, 'No one ever yet heard the divine pity except by lips that were moved by human pity'. Quite so. And you can be sure that where the human spirit is blocked and stifled, there is no chance that people will feel the presence of the Spirit of God. But isn't that exactly what they *need* to feel in those inevitable sadnesses? How 'Abide With Me' surrounded by chromium and plastic, whining electrics and Harry Secombe with a crack in the record?

Secondly, a man and wife in my parish had tried seven years to have a child. Eventually she became pregnant and all went well. The prognosis was a healthy child. But he died at birth, suffocated on the umbilical cord. This was at half-past five in the morning. At half-past seven the husband left his wife's bedside to enquire of the Ward Sister how he might go about arranging a funeral for his son. She told him he would have to wait until half-past nine when the Administration Block (an apt phrase) would open. So when the time came he went to beg the body. 'Leave it to us', said the administrator, 'and go back to your wife'. The administrator offered him an unseen 'disposal' and the burial of his child in a quiet corner of the municipal cemetery. My parishioner pressed for the release of the body. The administrator, who really was trying to be kind, said, 'I'm only trying to save you *unnecessary* grief'. He completely failed to see that grief was the only thing the young man needed to express. Grief was the only mode of expression left to him. Finally the administrator brought up his biggest disuasive cannon. 'It'll cost you money, you know.'

It may, of course, be alleged that these tribulations represent occasional lapses in the normally beneficent workings of a good system. But that is not my experience. Almost every critical encounter with institutionalized caring reveals some outstanding crassness. And yet with the crassness there is real concern among people in the professions who are genuinely trying to be of some use to the stricken. But individual acts of sensitivity and caring cannot flourish in a system which is inhuman. It is the context which is wrong, the mode of perceiving human need which has become warped by the intrusion of emotional clichés: the over-sumptuous garden at the crematorium; the nice music which, by association with other muzaks and the locations where these occur, turns nasty, a black comedy, sickly, surreal; the jargon of 'precipitation' and the instant production of tranquillizers for the relief of human feelings when the only way in which relief is possible is by the expression of those feelings; the definition of sudden bereavement as 'mild anxiety'; the desire to separate the living from the dead at the very instant of demise; the unwitting creation of a bedlam in which the emotionally disturbed housewife was placed as part of her treatment – it was called the 'Rest Room'. If we so arrange things that human beings *in extremis* are always brought into contact with a dehumanizing system, then we can be certain of one thing only: they will be dehumanized. Insensitivity is catching. The virus is all around. When we are treated insensitively, we behave insensitively, beget and nurture insensitive children, create newer and bigger institutions of even greater insensitivity until the whole civilization becomes a wilderness of official signs, bureaucratic procedures, methods, systems, files, printouts, case-numbers, codes and suffixes – all part of a jargon inimical to human beings who are made victims of administration blocks and end their days with unwitnessed disposal.

All is piecemeal, fragmentation. The cultural environment cannot sustain the human spirit, and therefore it cannot reveal the spirit of God, because it has no coherence, no cohesiveness. Because we live in a world of material, the cultural environment is mediated by physical objects arranged in space. Incarnation. Order and coherence give meaning to human thought and movement. That is why we are pleased by good architecture and interior design. It does not much matter whether this architecture or design happens to be Greek, Roman, Byzantine, Baroque or Municipal Gothic. I said, 'physical objects arranged in space'. That is, we must be able to perceive that some mind has gone into the arrangement. Without mind, order and form physical objects represent only what is haphazard. Chaos instead of cosmos. Animation, life in an environment exists only by the fusion of thought with thing. The absence of this fusion produces only confusion. We have no landmarks. All this is obvious enough. Why then does so much confusion and haphazardness exist? Why do we not perceive how we are being tricked out of our humanity by architectural and decorative speciousness? It is everywhere. There is only *one* environment, no living in the gallery or museum. Like Satan in the book of Job let us wander up and down on the face of the earth and see what there is to see.

Go in any pub. Muzak hits you as you enter and pass the electronic gaming machine which some person will be playing with the attitude of one assiduously desiring damnation. This is the world of operant conditioning. The bleeps, the whirring symbols, the few coins unloosed by the machine now and again like so many peanuts before Dr Skinner's pigeons. The bleeps make bad counterpoint with the muzak. The bar and the rest of the 'lounge' will be a confusion of oak and plastic. Genuine horsebrasses nailed to the wishing-well bar next to the digital reckoning machine for the darts. The jukebox by the side of a grandfather clock. Too much writing of the coy euphemistic sort, 'RU18' and 'Yer Tis', 'Braves' and 'Squaws'. Under the wooden shield which used to belong to the landlady's grandmother, and which bears a Latin inscription, there may be another notice such as, 'Please do not ask for credit as a punch in the mouth often offends'. We are in the realm of what is 'light' again, 'a bit of fun' like the children's programmes and the pop radio stations. As the pub fills up and the jukebox gets turned up, it becomes impossible to have what pubs once existed to guarantee: a private chat in a public house. Because the muzak is so loud and continuous, everyone must shout. Babel. The louder one shouts the less gets conveyed. But criticize this madness and you will be told you are being a spoilsport for, of course, people go to pubs to 'have a bit of fun', 'a good time'. And so 'a good time', and hence 'good' itself, becomes defined by criteria which are themselves sub-human – the prevention of ordinary conversation; the abolition of subtlety in glance, nuance and gesture; the human voice turned into something brash, monosyllabic, loudly sloganizing. What can be conveyed at that pitch, in that background? And where are we supposed to be? The country alehouse? Yes, if the old milk churn and the leaded fireplace are anything to go by. The casino? Dingly Dell under the wishing well bar? Computerland? A pop concert? We cannot tell where we are in this heap of broken images. And if we cannot tell *where* we are, we cannot know *who* we are since everywhere we are part of a context. If we cannot know who we are, we cannot know how to behave. So we end up joining the confusion. A coin in the jukebox, another in the gaming machine. Confusion worse confounded. Here and there we can find one or two pubs which are not like this, but they are very exceptional and, like the occasional programme of quality on television, they have no hope of being influential in the general miasma of insanity and noise.

Leave the pub, then. Perhaps you find yourself in a pretty Cotswold village, or at an historic seaside town on the spectacular Yorkshire coast, it may be Staithes or Robin Hood's Bay: there between the ancient rows of houses or on the hillside of picturesque but stout fishermen's cottages you will find double yellow lines daubed like lesions on the landscape. Just see how clearly they show up on the photographs! Is it beyond the wit of enlightened, modern, technological man to find some less obtrusive way to request No Parking? Those lines cover even such places as Fountains Abbey. We do more disgrace with our insensitivity than ever Henry the Eighth did with his bulldozers. And all this under the auspices of the National Trust and the National Parks Commission. But if the shepherds are hirelings . . .

Muzak, chromium, fluorescent light strips, bleeping cash registers, children's toys that make unpleasant and intrusive noises simply because the micro chip makes 'perpetual audible monitoring' possible. All these things are everywhere: the pub, the club, supermarket, launderette, doctor's waiting room, inter-city train, hairdresser's. The only places which seem not to be so possessed are banks where the religious task of counting money would perhaps be sent awry by noises. Mammon is a jealous god. His service, whatever else it may be, is never 'a bit of fun'.

Fragmentation and rampant individualism. But individuals are created as a result of interplay with their environment. We are made by our context. Everyone 'must be free to make up his own mind'. But, as C. H. Sisson said, 'Minds must actually be filled with something.' What will minds in our present cultural context be made up of? Where is the humanizing effect of humane literature in a world where our bestselling paperback authors produce stories about torture, masturbation and a pickled penis in a glass jar? Two holiday-makers subjected to butchery described in terms of eroticism and sado-masochism – that is the plot of the critically acclaimed *The Comfort of Strangers* by Ian McEwan. Martin Amis has produced similar stuff in *Other People* and in a more recent novel the name of which, I am happy to say, I have forgotten. And *The Times Literary Supplement* hails these writers as if they were the heirs and successors of Lawrence and Joyce. The critics began to like McEwan immediately he had written that book about the children who buried their mother in the backyard and spent the rest of the story cruelly brooding in an atmosphere of putrescence. *The Sunday Times Colour Magazine* featured a conversation between these literary geniuses in which the talk was of whether one should eat one's wife's afterbirth. And *The Sunday Times* is described as a 'quality paper' – like its sister *The Times* which these days covers its features pages with the sort of titillations and trivia to be found only in the gutter press twenty years ago: the sex life of 'superstars'; 'the anatomy of a glue-sniffer'; endless information about astrology and 'lesbian love'; extensive coverage of 'rock, pop and media' as if these were the sorts of diversions to be sought after. *The Times* devotes space to a eulogy about Mr Terry Wogan the disc jockey who has graduated to the role of chat show host; gives encouragement to those who are still commercially exploiting the seven-years-dead Elvis Presley; has a full page on 'the magic of gadgets'; an article about President Reagan's wife Nancy which is written with a degree of effusiveness sufficient to have disgraced a better quality woman's magazine twenty years ago. Another piece: 'The Peacock Male: Action Man Strong and Stylish' – with pictures. At least *The Times* has not yet fallen to the level of the 'popular' dailies which ever more perfectly substitute grunts, slogans and interjections for words and sentences, and which have so refined the technique of putting the juiciest rape stories next to the pictures of their sexiest models that page after page is only pornography. Newspapers shape public opinion. Considered opinion can be expressed only in decent prose, not in grunts and exclamations. This is a further blow to the idea of an informed reading public. And a newspaper which can be as lurid and trivial as *The Mirror* or *The Sun* (or even as *The Times*) on its features pages will not inspire us to take much notice of what is said on the leader page. Show us what you value and we shall tell you what you are worth. What price the papers, then, as examples of society's public conversation? Are these things what we most want to talk about? – sex crimes, pop stars, bingo and astrology, venereal disease, lesbianism, gadgets and 'the changing image of President Reagan's not-so-loved leading lady'?

All is 'image' these days as reality is endlessly modified and disguised by fashion. We have forgotten the prohibition about the worship of images. Images cannot will or act; they are only perceived. So, if we define ourselves in terms of our images, we manufacture our own impotence and underline our amorality. Not every novel that comes out is as bad as those of McEwan and Martin Amis, although those writers are well supported by others such as Emma Tennant and D. M. Thomas in the production of sex, sadism and psychedelia, but the bestsellers create the ethos and the ethos determines the trade, which produces the readership, which demands more of the same. More newspeak: 'adult fiction', 'adult videos' – when these are the epithets by which addicts recognize new specimens of lurid immaturity. Not every newspaper goes in for sex and bingo, but those which do not quickly have 'circulation problems'. For circulation problems try healthy exercise and a better diet.

The 1944 Education Act envisaged the continuing moral and religious education of our children in state schools, but this is now generally of such poor quality, because based on incoherent educational and theological principles, that it does more harm than good. Advisers and teachers have inherited, along with everyone else, the fashionable pseudo-scientific world-view to be described in Chapter 3. This emerges in the form of exquisite agnosticism, a liberal prejudice so all-embracing as to be devoid of all affirmation save the affirmation that there are no spiritual realities and it is therefore certainly not the job of the RE 'specialist' to try to teach them. I have taught in and visited many schools. I have read the reports and the local authority syllabuses. There is a remarkable degree of consensus amounting almost to unanimity but for the awkward presence of a handful of fundamentalists in RE departments up and down the land.

The received wisdom in today's RE is that the teachers should teach everything and nothing, for the idea has got about that religion is such a touchy subject for modern man in his contemporary enlightenment that no self-respecting RE teacher dare suggest Christianity is actually true. Advisers and 'resource persons' – the present day Scribes – will all agree that religion can be a 'valid option' (the influence of consumerism again) or 'an appropriate stance for living' (there is something negative about that word 'stance' which, in the context, makes it insincere – puts it alongside those other unrealities 'role' and 'image') but, when it comes to the question of truth, they pass by on the other side. But what can be 'valid' if it is not true? How 'appropriate' is a 'stance' that is built on insecure foundation? RE teaching is like the supermarket, a religious bazaar in which the pupil can sample not only Christianity, Hinduism and Islam but Shamanism, Voodoo and Witchcraft. Take a little of each, for a bit of what you fancy does you good. 'Some people believe so and so . . . others believe such and such.' No 'why' about it. All religions can be treated as equally important in the received wisdom which regards them all as false. However, insults to past traditions have a habit of rebounding in the present and future, as we shall see.

Voodoo, fertility cults, astrology, numerology and the Tarot. Bermuda Triangle, God was a spaceman, and arcane ruminations about whether Lot's wife was turned into a pillar of salt in a nuclear explosion. 'Interesting speculation that, Sharon; it shows the relevance of the connection between our religious education module and modern weapons systems.' Others study, for CSE projects, the cults of unreason such as Divine Light, the Children of God and the bacchanalia of the Orange People under the direction of their silent guru with the fifty white Rolls Royce cars. Are we supposed to believe that children – children of 'the low ability range' at that – in the middle forms of the Secondary School are able to deal adequately with movements that beguile their older brothers and sisters in university?

On the one hand, educational experts tell us how impressionable young people are, but in the matter of RE these same young people are expected to possess powers of judgement to which few adults would aspire. I refer to the local authorities' Agreed Syllabuses. Upper Juniors in Sunderland, for example, study the life of Krishna and it is said that this will require consideration of 'Indus Valley civilization, life and customs of India, some notion of reincarnation and the role [what else!] of Brahmins'. Is this before or after morning playtime, I wonder? In fact, the nine year old is going to be at it all day because he will find that Muhammad and Buddha are on the syllabus as well. In the case of Muhammad he is asked to pay particular attention to the prophet's attack on polytheism; in the case of Buddha he must study that Founder's previous lives and enlightenment.

Who is being enlightened here? No one. For the Junior School pupil is only confused by being asked to set these stories of eastern gods and prophets beside the story of Jesus. He will want to know – and I have heard it asked – 'Which story is true?' and 'Is Lord Krishna a Lord like Lord

Jesus?' It is at this moment, of course, that the RE teacher is supposed to perform his vanishing trick, for truth has no part in this sort of education, only opinion: and the nine year old must be 'allowed to make up his own mind'. To make up his own mind on the basis of *what*? And the answer is liberal prejudice and the secular utilitarian superstition that all religions are of equal value, that they are all the same kind of thing and can be studied as 'units' in the same 'course' – labelled and stored under various 'project headings', analysed as part of the 'input' to the RE module in the humanities faculty. There is no humanity in it. 'We did Buddha in the autumn, Sir; and, after Christmas, we're going to do Jesus.' This is a kind of mindless arrogance which amounts to brainwashing with liberal values – values which are never questioned, never scrutinized as closely as the various religions which are so airily 'packaged', dismissed or otherwise got rid of. Moreover, it is a thoroughly sham liberalism since it tolerates religion only up to that point at which any adherent might want to claim it as true or even as important in his daily life and so start to offend against the totalitarian blandness of liberalism itself. If anyone doubts this, he has only to consider the controversy which arose in Bradford when Muslims wanted to have their meat slaughtered according to Islamic ritual. Or he can look at a dozen other flashpoints which occur as soon as anyone starts to take his religion seriously in our so-tolerant society.

The contemporary babel in RE begins from impeccable motives. In its comparative religion course, the Wiltshire Agreed Syllabus sets out to enable pupils 'to enter, as deeply as possible and without premature evaluation, into the feelings, beliefs and actions of the believer'. This aim, laudable as it sounds, is mistaken in principle. On the basis of *what* can a person 'from the 13-plus range' possibly enter into the nature of four or five religions in this way? Those of us who have tried know that it is difficult enough to enable a child to acquire the feel of even one faith, and that Christianity. The truth is that religion is cultural. True religion is what is taken most seriously by its practitioners. It is what one most strongly believes about everything one does. It is what is discovered in the depths, what cannot be denied because its symbolic language transcends and incorporates the very syzygy of affirmation-denial. It is what binds a man. What would it mean to be bound to something as tenuous as the content of the pile of syllabuses on my desk? What would it mean to practise a religion that was only comparatively true?

By lumping all the religions together in this way, contemporary RE reveals what it regards as the one true religion: secular utilitarianism and technologico-Benthanism by which all the so-called 'religions' can be evaluated and allotted a place in the timetable. This secular overview is regarded as absolutely true in our society and so no one is allowed to question it. This bland totalitarianism advertises itself as 'pluralism' and 'tolerance' but it only tolerates what it has already rejected as primitive and unscientific, out of step with the way enlightened secularists see the world. It is as if the leaders in RE are saying, 'Let them study religion. It can't do any harm since we know it's not true – and no one takes it seriously anyhow.'

But there is no neutral point from which pupils can learn about all religions. The assumption that there is such a point leads to the conclusion that all religions are false. That neutral point becomes the opening credal statement of the religion of pseudo-scientific relativism. Religion cannot be something that is learned *about* without its becoming something other than religion. Religion can only be learned through the observance of regular feasts and fasts, the learning by heart and frequent recitation of Scriptures and prayers and the gradual coming to feel the significance of these customs and actions to the life of every day. Minds must actually be filled with something. Christian religion will only be taught again in this country when there is a renascence of English cultural tradition. Otherwise it will remain forever what it is now – a more or less interesting historical subject, an 'option' which some people 'even today' find 'valid' or 'appropriate' as 'a stance for life'. To adopt the style of the sloganizers: Absolute Relativism Rules OK. Cathedrals and ornaments thus become only interesting archaeological remains of a dead culture, like the old shield in the trendy pub: 'This is what people *used to be* concerned with.' 'This is what primitive people believed in the olden days.' Always the disparaging note as if the modern age knows best. But Augustine, Aquinas, Donne, Cranmer, Bishop Berkeley, Hopkins, Eliot, *primitive*? They should see us now! In short, if the modern age is so right in theory, why is it so obviously wrong in practice? It cannot provide the personal and psychological means for the putting into words and actions those deep feelings of love and death, of suffering, awe, loss and redemption. It can give no meaning beyond what is trivial to those archetypal experiences which created the art and literature of Christian tradition. So, outside the ghetto of high culture we inhabit a world which is trivial, noisy and brash. Dissociation is the norm. It is the new Babel in which every new idea is instantaneously out of date. Nothing follows nothing except more fast talk and ever-decreasing seriousness. Because we cared nothing for it, the glory has departed. Because we did not attend, did not concentrate on the perpetual necessity of putting our deepest human feelings into words and making the environment both reflect and renew them, we discover – if we discover anything at all – that we have invented a waste land without cultural landmarks of any sort. We did not incarnate the spirit and so the spirit has gone from us. We were told a long time ago that it blows where it wills.

How to live in such a waste? What hope of reconstruction? These are desperate issues.

3
Faith in the Age of Technology

Our predicament: we need faith but faith is impossible. God is dead and it is the modern scientific world outlook which has killed him. And yet this desire for inward peace, a sense of meaning and belonging, persists in us. We feel cheated. How unfair that we should have this longing when the means for its satisfaction is only an illusion! Since there is no God, our desire for faith seems to us an example of bad faith, wishful thinking, mere hypocrisy. And the modern secular world tells us to leave behind that childish desire, that ontological fiction called God, and to get on with the real business of living – to immerse ourselves in useful activity, to be concerned with the issues of the day, to find a constructive morality without God. God is a dream from our infancy. We must 'come of age' as Bonhoeffer put it.

When I was a boy I possessed at all times the certainty of God's existence. This certainty did not make me more moral, better than the other boys, but it was a kind of deep security. I felt that God really did exist beyond the bright blue sky, that he was behind the world of time and flux supporting everything, giving to the whole universe its cause, reason and purpose. In my teens I met the usual atheistic and agnostic arguments. At first, these were crudely expressed. 'If God exists, *where* is he?' This objection was soon dispatched: of course you could not hope to locate God in that way, as if he were one more member of the universe of species. Curates and paperback apologies for the Christian faith taught me to say that God is beyond time and space, that eternity is not simply endless time, that God is spirit and so on. In my naive confidence it never occurred to me to wonder if there was not something bogus about talking of God's being outside space and time. It was only later that I felt the full force of the sceptical argument: 'You can't talk about a *being* who is beyond space and time, because our whole use of the word 'being' demands space and time. To say that God exists beyond space and time simply means that he exists nowhere and never. And that means you cannot talk about his existence.'

The escape from scepticism could only be achieved by the invocation of metaphysics, of a realm that was beyond this world and which acts as the explanation and origin of this world. Then they told me about Occam's Razor. This is a philosophical principle which says, 'Entities should not be multiplied beyond what is strictly necessary.' What was the point of inventing a metaphysical world in order to explain this world? That only led to further problems when we came to the need to explain the metaphysical world. 'God made everything', says the defender of faith. 'Then who made God?' asks the blunt sceptic. To claim that God does not need an explanation, that he is himself his own explanation, is simply not to play fair. It is a last ditch attempt to define God into existence as that which is its own explanation. But why should I believe that such a God exists? Where is the evidence? If I reply, 'Well, because the world exists, it must be created and sustained by God', I am met by the response, 'No. There is no need for God as the explanation; scientific understanding can lead us to all the explanations we need.' The atheist goes further and claims that, in a world without God, scientific explanations are the only sort of explanations available. Attempts to produce other, metaphysical, explanations only result in confusion and incoherence. The beards of wishful-thinking theologians are shaved by Occam's Razor. We must learn to grow up and cope with the world as it is. And it is not a world charmed or haunted by divinities. It is a puzzle nonetheless – but it is a puzzle which science will solve, is solving already.

And what wonders science has brought forth: cars, aeroplanes, space-travel, radio, television, microcomputers; and, among many blessings, anaesthetics, antibiotics, surgery, immunization, disinfectant, open heart operations and cures and so on. Moreover, all these things have been achieved by the very *method* of science. They are examples which justify scientific principles. Science really is telling us what the world is like and how it works. Who can doubt the authority of science when its method has brought such tangible and spectacular results? Who nowadays could argue for a world of gods, demons and enchantment in the face of so much real achievement by a method which denies those ghosts and replaces them with a world of molecules and microbes, of electrical currents and sub-atomic particles?

So why do we not acquiesce in this scientific world? Why do we not learn to accept it; even, using our old-fashioned religious sense, to give a sort of secular thanks for it? It can make us comfortable, enlarge the scope of our opportunities and provide us with both an absorbing interest and a task. It can supply more achievable moral ends than religion. For, while we find it psychologically impossible to love a non-existent God and morally vague to love our neighbour as ourself, we can actually do a bit of real, physical good with the aid of scientific knowledge: we can use the discoveries of science to make everyone's life more comfortable, happier, by the provision of cheap food, warmth, travel, hospital care and other forms of social welfare. Surely to hanker after God when we have all these things is dishonest, superstitious, crying for the moon? Well, we can have the moon, too – thanks to science.

Of course, growing up is a painful experience. We keep backsliding into childish ways. But with the help of education we shall surely overcome these childish temptations to rely on ancient superstitions. We shall learn to smile at the idea of God just as the adult smiles at the idea of Santa Claus. We shall learn to be satisfied with scientific explanations because these are the only realistic explanations, the only explanations which can be of any use to us. To want God back again is an unworthy desire. Science teaches us that we can stand on our own feet. Therefore we are morally obliged to do so and to refuse illusory comforts. Much better to direct our attention and efforts to the improvement of scientific understanding so that the benefits of science may be increased and universally applied. And so the scientific criticism of faith is not only an intellectual criticism but a moral one. 'You *cannot* take comfort in ancient suppositions' implies 'You *ought* not to take comfort in them.'

The very practice of religion is an abomination to the scientific outlook. All that creeping into church and moaning about one's faults – it is so useless, unproductive. It gets nothing done, makes no improvements to our lives. Time and money spent on obeisance to an illusion. What is religion but an institutionalized evasion of our responsibilities? Doing, helping, working is better than praying for the unfortunate. It may be objected: 'Many who pray also work and help.' 'Very well – let them stop praying and use the time for working harder, with more dedication.' And science can claim that its moral imperatives in no way fall short of the demands of religion, for science urges us to strive, to commit our whole being to the cause, to care about others and to bend our intelligence and will to the betterment of man's life.

Still we feel there is something missing and we are not convinced by the assertion that what we crave is only an illusory comfort. We may agree that science has destroyed the credibility of God beyond space and time but what else has science destroyed? Science objects to the religious view of man as flawed creature, dependent on the mysterious grace of Almighty God for his life and destiny, but the scientific view of man is even more objectionable. For all his talk about the use of science to improve man's life, the scientist cannot get away from the message which emanates from the theoretical centre of his own discipline, the vision of man created by science: it is the vision of man as molecules and mechanism. Science regards man as a machine with moving parts, governed by the latest version of the laws of electro-chemistry. When the scientist wants to talk about man's moral responsibility, his obligation to use science to improve our fortunes, he is obliged to forsake the candour of scientific thought and invent a ghost in the machine. For molecules and chemicals do not make moral choices. Machines may, in some automatic, serial, programmed fashion, 'think' but they are not human. When the scientist regards the basic structure of man as mechanical, he redefines what it is to be a man.

It is not pollution, chemical warfare and the hydrogen bomb which make up the curse of science, it is the nature and methodology of pure science itself which is so destructive, such a perversion of what was formerly understood by the term 'man'. Charles Dickens saw this in Gradgrind and statistics, facts, the subordination of human nature to an abstraction, the slavery of human beings not just to individual machines but to the very idea of mechanism. The same objection, updated and intensified, is there in D. H. Lawrence's hatred for the mechanization even of intimacy, desire and spasm. It is there in Huxley's dystopia *Brave New World* – not only in the test-tube babies, but in the notion that man must be remade in the form of a race predetermined, without choices. If science wants to put itself on the side of what is noble in mankind, it must abandon its own procedures and borrow a different idea of man – that is to say, a religious idea. For progress and enlightenment are not the only conditions that can be predicted for machines; define man as mechanism and you will more likely end up with a totalitarian technology like 1984 than with a world of sweetness and light. The point is that scientific methodology is neutral with regard to social and ethical results. *Mechanism gives no place to morality.* This point needs to be stressed because the competence of scientific method to provide ethical imperatives is very rarely challenged. It is simply assumed that scientific enterprise is, give or take a few thousand hydrogen bombs, 'good'. I am only pointing out that the scientific method, which regards its basic material as molecules and mechanism, *cannot* generate ethics of any sort.

Religion and science have different sets of vocabulary, tell different stories about what it is to be a man. For the one, we are 'frail children of dust' yet made in the image of God; sinners yet saved; mortal yet destined to put on immortality; members of Christ, children of God and inheritors of the Kingdom of Heaven. For the other, we are atoms and plasma, genes and chromosomes, reflexes both conditioned and unconditioned. The two stories cannot be merged. It makes no sense to talk about genes making choices or about reflexes committing sins. The really thoroughgoing scientific reformer is not sorry about this. He has no longing to return to the religious story, for it is a story which is simply not true. But what kind of truth are we talking about here? The only sort of truth which is of any practical use is the truth that enables us to make sense of our experience. Ironically, that is also one of the basic claims of science and called 'empiricism'; but the scientist will admit only a narrow range of basic concepts as necessary to a definition of experience. The ordinary man willingly accepts the scientist's teaching about atoms and molecules, genes and electro-chemicals. But – and this is crucial – he regards such teaching as irrelevant to his everyday life, to what really matters to him, to his experience.

It is part of the condition of man that he needs to say

things which cannot be said in scientific language. He wants to talk about love, hate, hope, fear, joy and wonder. He may even want to talk about a sense of inadequacy and guilt, of a sense of his own individuality and calling, of 'heart' and 'soul'. When he does talk about these things, annoyingly persisting in talking about them even after two hundred years of scientific progress, he must adopt a language which is not that of the scientific method. The question then arises: is this language of fear and hope, love and dread, real or illusory, false or true? Is it a legitimate, serious way of talking, or is it only a set of shadows from the superstitious past? Is it only 'nice' and 'comfortable' but not true? Does it only hover above the hard realities like some dubious ectoplasm?

In practice these questions never arise, of course. We do not really doubt the value and significance of the unscientific language. It is what we live by, what makes us what we are. We accept scientific explanations as information about how things work. But we use the unscientific language when we wish to speak about all those things that are of most importance to us, including our close relationships with others. Science can explain how we tick, but there is another expression, 'what makes us tick', which has nothing at all to do with mechanism. Now, it makes no sense to say that those things which are most important to us do not exist. The old, unscientific, religious words do point to something beyond themselves, they do refer; and the reference is our lives. No one doubts the usefulness of scientific language but, while most purposes could proceed happily without words like 'biochemical', 'molecule' and 'operant conditioning', it is difficult to see how anything remotely similar to human life could proceed without such words as 'love', 'fear', 'awe' and 'wonder'. The unscientific language is valid because any accusation of its invalidity results in absurdity. We know in our experience minute by minute that life is like *this*.

The substitution of scientific language for the theological—emotional mode of speech has, in certain key areas, resulted in the impoverishment of human life. Language about genes cannot do the work of language about choices. Reflexes, conditioned or otherwise, cannot do justice to our sense of morality. So one of the main areas of our impoverishment has been and is the result of the attempt to invent 'scientific ethics'. This emerged in the work of Jeremy Bentham's brand of utilitarianism where the scientific notions are paramount as Bentham talks of measuring pain and pleasure according to his 'utilitarian calculus'. The words of that version of ethics really belong in the scientific textbook: there is talk of *maximizing* pleasure and *minimizing* pain when we all know that the words 'maximum' and 'minimum' belong in the equation or on the graph paper. Ethics becomes quantity instead of quality. Value becomes something measurable. This is not only mechanism, it is an inversion and a subversion of original meanings: for what could possibly *measure* value when value itself is precisely the measure in ethical cases?

The scientific vocabulary has exceeded its proper limits until the whole world, including human beings themselves, has become construed as a machine. Even psychology, which originally meant the study of the soul, has been turned into a science. Human subjects are scarcely dignified with personality but referred to as 'organisms' without passion or self-understanding but with 'drives', 'instincts' and 'reflexes'. All is 'motivation', 'extinction' and 'conditioning'; desires become 'disorders of affect'; thinking is a mechanical, measurable 'process' called 'cognition'; pain is only 'negative reinforcement'; the mechanics of 'perception' involve 'factor analysis' interpreted by 'correlation coefficients'; intelligence has its 'quotient' and the mind itself is an interaction of 'stimulus and response'. This sort of language is what 'operates' and 'functions' in the psychology departments of all the universities. It is not even a caricature of human beings – for even a caricature has character – but a diagram. There are things to be said about what it is to be human which cannot be expressed in the vocabulary of the psychology laboratory. And these are the most human things. So modern psychology, based as it is on science, does not tell us what we might look to it to tell us: it tells us nothing about what it is to be human. But the scientific language is, here also, the language which is held to be most true, most accurate, most reliable; and the older language which was frankly spiritual is regarded by all the best people as 'outdated' and 'unverifiable'. But which language tells us what we want and need to know about human beings, that of Shakespeare and Dante or that of the psychology textbook?

In every area of human experience the scientific language has taken over, and it has failed to do what the older, personal and spiritual language did. It does not add to understanding but only trivializes it. Even (especially) the most personal and intimate aspects of our lives are invaded and subverted by sterile, mechanical jargon. Sex becomes a 'technique' – like operating a capstan lathe. In a BBC programme about 'sex therapy' there was talk of relationships having 'broken down' as if the estate of matrimony were a Ford car; there was reference to 'a specific therapeutic tool' (*sic*); an 'analysis' which went 'from one end of the spectrum to the other'; 'the body *worked*'; a woman was 'all screwed up'; there was talk of 'sexual malfunction'. It is possible to talk about sex like this, of course. But to do so is no longer to talk about anything human. The ultimate perversion is linguistic.

Education is organized on scientific principles: children's abilities – their 'capacities' and 'performances' – are analysed, correlated, measured and assessed. In Oxford there is even a laboratory for the measurement of 'religious response'; typically it is called a 'unit' – part of a chain, a sequence, a column of numbers; and experiences are evaluated 'on a scale'. Where would a resurrection appearance fit on that scale? Would Abraham's terror at the command to sacrifice his son come further up or lower down than Isaiah's dread in the temple when he saw the Lord, 'high and lifted up' and heard the words of the Sanctus? No part of life untouched by ghastly mechanism, the argot of axle, lever and pulley, the constraints of the graph and the drawing board. The coming of microcomputers is accelerating and intensifying this mutation of humanity from sentient being to bag of numbers.

The old language was rejected, remember, because it was held to be false; it presented a way of looking at the world which was based on illusion, delusion, wishful thinking and primitive superstition. This old language included wonder and awe, fear and dread, love and hate and, of course, God. And God had to be rejected before all the rest because his existence was 'unverifiable'. But this was verification construed in a very narrow sense: it meant that God was not susceptible to scientific investigation. He could not be seen, measured, evaluated. He would not show up in the telescope or the microscope or on the radar screen. Well, the Bible told us as much, 'no man has seen God at any time'. God could not be located as a phenomenon among phenomena, as a cause among causes. He was not an old man in the sky. He could not be discovered metaphysically, 'behind' the world. There was no need of him as an 'hypothesis'. But the rejection of God was the beginning of the loss of a whole history of a way of regarding mankind. The idea of God is hardly recoverable nowadays because almost everyone conspires to make this idea into a nonsense, and churchmen both conservative and liberal are the chief offenders.

In the nineteenth century there was a continuous squabble between conservative Christians and others, within and outside the Church, who supported the new scientific ideas not just of Charles Darwin and the evolutionists but of a long list of 'progressive' thinkers from Bentham and Mill to Comte, Feuerbach and Herbert Spencer. Liberal clergymen were attacked in public and more than 100,000 laity and 11,000 clergy brought a charge against Williams and Wilson who had written essays in the radical volume *Essays and Reviews* denying the fact of eternal punishment for the damned. It strikes us as astonishing from this distance in time that these men were convicted by the Ecclesiastical Court. However, the House of Lords reversed the decision on appeal and Williams and Wilson were released. There was more than a touch of humour to lighten these bizarre events: a wit remarked that the Lord Chancellor had 'dismissed Hell with costs and taken away from orthodox members of the Church of England their last hope of everlasting damnation'. The conservatives were furious and they became ever more extreme insisting on the literal accuracy of the Adam and Eve story and attributing the enormous longevity of the Patriarchs – more than nine hundred years in some cases – to 'great purity of life'. The Old Testament account itself does not always seem to support that judgement! There occurred the rise of fundamentalism with all its absurdities and obscurities. As the scientific knowledge, and the liberalizing, relativizing spirit that went with it, progressed, thousands turned against the Church as out of date, reactionary, a dissonance in the *Zeitgeist*.

But the fundamentalists in the Church could not avoid being affected by the scientific method. They were driven into a defensive attitude which envisaged God as one more example of scientifically described causation. This was a mechanical God who was called upon to fill every gap in scientific knowledge. God intervened by miracles to answer prayer, suspending the so called 'laws of nature' when necessary. The Bible came to be seen as an alternative scientific account to be set beside that of the evolutionists. Science and religion became rival explanations not only of human psychology but of the origin of causation in the physical universe.

The fundamentalists could not see that they had simply appropriated the literal mechanicalism of science and applied it to God. They were prisoners of an analogy, a faulty analogy at that. Their intelligence was 'bewitched by the abuse of language', as Wittgenstein used to say. God was a being among other beings, infinitely wise and of endless power but a being none the less. So God's existence became a matter for evidences and verification as theologians in the fundamentalist mould argued for the necessity of the divine being in exactly the same way as a Newtonian mechanic argued for the necessity of gravity in order to explain why apples fall to the ground. While consciously opposing modern science, the fundamentalists unconsciously adopted the scientific method. And so they created the quasi-physical God, distant metaphysical cousin to the Old Man in the sky of popular superstition. It was inevitable that the putative existence of this God should be dismissed as a grammatical fiction by the twentieth-century heirs of the nineteenth-century positivists: the logical positivists. How could such a mechanism as the fundamentalists' God ever do service for the true God who is 'Thou' to the psalmist and who is called 'the Father of our Lord Jesus Christ'? Wittgenstein again: 'If the existence of such a being were ever to be proved, I should feel obliged to oppose him.'

The liberal theologians, too, are in the grip of the same faulty analogy. Their 'technique' is to disown the grosser aspects of literal-mindedness but still to find room for 'a God who acts'. Beggared by scientific notions about causation and action, the liberals succeed only in creating a God who is so attenuated that his existence would seem hardly to matter. The God of Pannenberg and Küng, of Karl Rahner and Professor Wiles is truly ghostly, but not in the haunting fashion of the presence which made Jacob cry out 'How dreadful is this place'; only ghostly like an epiphenomenon, ectoplasm, what J. A. T. Robinson once called 'the last fading smile of a cosmic Cheshire cat'.

Because the liberals are concerned to defend the being of God against the attacks of science, they fail to do justice to the original experiences which called forth biblical prose and the religious poetry and prayers of such as John Donne and St Augustine. Whoever those men, saints and geniuses, thought they were addressing, it was no being alongside beings, a quasi-physical entity forever lurking behind the clouds, a stop-gap for all the failed explanations of science. The God of the spiritual man is spiritual. That is to say he is within. The Kingdom of God is within you.

In our present age no one wants to know about a God who is a spiritual reality – because the scientific prejudice has made us believe that spiritual things are not really real. We prefer the quasi-physical being, the mechanism. At least we can reject that and talk about our period as a 'faithless era'. But the true God can never be so disposed of for he is a description – and more than a description, an apprehension – of certain inevitabilities which take place in the depths of our personality, or, as the age of faith would have said, 'soul'. This spiritual God is the God of the psalmist who, when he sang:

> Oh Lord, thou hast searched me out and known me:
> Thou knowest my downsitting and mine uprising;
> Thou understandest my thoughts long before . . .
> Whither shall I go from thy Spirit
> Or whither shall I flee from thy presence?

was not thinking of some cosmic apparition in the galactic flux.

There is, of course, an externality about religious language but this arises because we are obliged to talk about what there is, things. We are makers of metaphors and poems. Isaiah in the temple was not terrified by a vision that might have been a drawing on the wall: he was disturbed by his encounter with an inner, spiritual reality and his ecstatic poem of praise – 'Mine eyes have seen the King, the Lord of Hosts' – was a verbal eruption from the depths of that inner turmoil. The external, propositionalized event is a projection of an inner reality. It is not, in the jargon of sceptical banality, 'only a projection'; it is the true objective – correlative of what is spiritually true. The experience creates the vision or the poem and in our turn we are led from an acquaintance with the vision or the poem to apprehend the experience. Words and pictures are sacramental signs.

We do not 'verify' the existence of God within us according to methods invented by science and logical positivism. We do not need abstract arguments in order to demonstrate the 'being' of God. We learn his nature through direct experience in our inner lives and pre-eminently by attending to words, music and pictures which our apprehension of him has led us to produce. As we study the art and literature of western culture we come to see that the deepest and most human experiences have created sacred and classic texts. For example, it may be said of the Psalms what was once extravagantly claimed for a Sunday newspaper: all human life is there. The ecstasy of thanksgiving and praise called forth out of our awe and wonder at creation: 'The heavens are telling the glory of God and the firmament showeth his handiwork.' Despair and panic when we feel the absence of God: 'Out of the deep'; 'My God, why hast thou forsaken me?' The comfort and encouragement of order both natural and moral: 'The law of the Lord is an undefiled law converting the soul.' Disease, betrayal, bereftness, suffering, death, salvation, new life and hope – these are first of all experiences which happen to human beings. Sacred texts give them their most authentic reference. It is the depth of human feeling allied with fierce and sustained powers of concentration which produces these texts. They are, as Eliot said of poetry, 'raids on the articulate'. They do not drop neatly out of the sky into the ready hands of fanatics who are misled so far as to mistake sanctimoniousness for inspiration. They are hewn out of the hard rock of human life and suffering.

Well, it may be objected that there is no necessity upon us to claim that these texts, profound though they may be, originate from God. But the objector is still thinking of God 'the being' and it is that misguiding concept which provides the grounds for the objection. It is more profitable to turn the argument round and see in the God language the best expression of all those deep human experiences of fullness and emptiness, love and death. It is ludicrous to argue that the Psalms contain great spiritual and psychological insights but that it is a pity these insights were expressed in the God language! If they could have been expressed more adequately in another sort of language, then they would have been so expressed and that other expression would be remembered and treasured and the Psalms forgotten.

The power of the original poetic response together with generations when the poems are hallowed by time and use create what is sacred about these texts. The words are not ordinary words, mundane; they radiate a numinous power. They are at once familiar and strange. They attract and they repel. They are, literally, words which overcome the world precisely because they express the world perfectly and so transcend it. They are not 'only words' but somehow solid, embodiments of what it is to live, suffer and rejoice as a human being. Their profundity makes them into religious symbols – that is, archetypal representations which are full of health-giving, redeeming power because they unite and transcend the contradictions and inner oppositions which occur throughout the rest of our experience. An analogy: a religious symbol in words, pictures or music is like a three-dimensional object which displays all its planes simultaneously. A religious symbol gives meaning to the flux of life's events in something like the way a symphony makes whole music out of particular cacophonies and dissonances. Indeed, the dissonances are vital – a fact of musical aesthetics which has application for the study of the nature of religious expression.

Of course, the form of religious expression is always changing along with general changes in sensibility and temper. It is a different age which produced the Psalms from the one which produced *The Waste Land*. The Psalms will always remain sacred texts but there are modern works which are monuments to profound religious expression. It may not be quite right to describe these as sacred texts, because one of the most important changes in modern sensibility involves uneasiness with the idea of the sacred itself. But, if we are looking for the same criteria as before – intense experience at the deepest human level allied to fierce and sustained power of concentration – then we shall not hesitate to claim such as *Four Quartets*, *Also Sprach Zarathustra* and the trilogy of novels by Samuel Beckett for modern spiritual classics. The form of expression has changed but the fundamental human experiences behind that expression remain the same. The psalmist speaks of 'going heavily', 'the valley of the shadow' and the God who has absented himself. Beckett writes about boredom and worry, tedium and the sense of being oppressed by nothingness. These are different expressions of a recognizably similar experience. Why does the shift so often seem so great? Why won't the words of the psalmist stand alone for all time as a summary of human experience? There is no easy answer but part of the reason must lie within the nature of human experience itself and the developments in the language which necessarily follow new experiences. The scientific world view is such a development and no modern writer can afford to ignore it if he wants to speak to his contemporaries. As we saw in the early part of this chapter in the difficulties with the word 'God', science has led to a kind of objectifying of experience. So a modern writer's style, his means of expression, will reflect this change and, for example, his sense of loneliness will no longer be expressed in the felt subjectivity of 'God's absence' but it will likely emerge in the form of an objective proposition – 'God does not exist'. (Take account of Frege and Russell's work on the logic of predication and it soon becomes clear that a technical device – the 'theory of descriptions' – becomes necessary even to deny the existence of God!)

When Nietzsche announced 'God is dead!' it was a religious act. It was the objectified form of God's felt absence in the Psalms and in a mystical tradition which includes Gregory of Nyssa and St John of the Cross. And Nietzsche's atheistic book *Also Sprach Zarathustra* is a religious text, for the writer is not merely expressing the non-existence of God as a formal, academic proposition; he is putting into poetic articulation in the language of his time the forsakenness of the psalmist or of Christ on the cross. Reading *Zarathustra* no one can doubt Nietzsche's religious intensity. He is also among the prophets. His words do not spring from the same source as the glib utopians, positivists and utilitarian calculators such as Comte, Feuerbach and Bentham. (It is instructive to note that when Auguste Comte asked George Eliot to write a 'Positivist Utopia' she replied with a poem, *O May I Join the Choir Invisible?*) Nietzsche's personality and writings reveal him as a great and deep religious thinker, a man who lived and wrote his actual terrors and delights. His words have about them the same numinous intensity as the Psalms or the Collects from the Book of Common Prayer. It is no use trying to write him off as 'an atheist': his ideas are variations on the themes central to the psalmist's absent God and to the dereliction expressed by Job. It may be said of Nietzsche what he himself said of Mozart: 'Inferior men should not be allowed even to praise him.'

Nietzsche's atheism and Samuel Beckett's nihilism should not be confused with the diagrammatic, positivistic atheism of the scientific world view. Those writers and others like them – Eliot in *The Waste Land*, Joyce in *Ulysses*, Lawrence in *Women in Love* – have given expression to human depths. And one thing at least is clear and ought to be so even to the most glib religious enthusiast: no one who has not visited those depths and felt the barrenness and forsakenness which reside near the centre of human experience should be allowed to speak to us of God.

Religious texts are dialogues between faith and doubt, dark and light, love and death – ingredients, as Goethe said, of any successful drama. They must be found to contain not only bright-eyed affirmation and unimpeded certainty but also loss, dejection, denunciation and despair – *must* because if they are to function as religious symbols they are bound to contain and express the opposite poles of human experience. Symbols are by nature paradoxical. They are emblems and images. Stories, too, are abiding images of all human life, and in the next chapter I want to look to the place of stories in religion and to trust fiction to tell us the truth.

4
Stories that Save us

Is the parable of the Good Samaritan true? I mean 'true' in
the literal sense. Did a 'certain man' in fact go 'down from
Jerusalem to Jericho' and fall among thieves? Was it a real
priest, a real Levite who 'passed by on the other side'? And
was it indeed left to a real historical Samaritan to bind up
the wounds of the stricken traveller, put him on his own
beast and pay his lodging at the inn? Or was the whole
story simply made up by Jesus or even by the writer of St
Luke's Gospel? Most people would agree that the story of
the Good Samaritan was an invention to aid teaching and
that its literal truth or falsity could never dull its moral
impact in the slightest. But why do we value stories above
precepts? Why do religious teachers, why did Jesus, insist
on storytelling as an essential part of teaching? Why not
stick to rules, commandments, principles?

We may perhaps answer that stories are a lot more
interesting than abstract formulations about duty, rights
and conduct. All sermons are more or less boring, but any
preacher will confirm that the parts of his sermons which
attract most interest are those in which he tells an anec-
dote, a joke, a story. The preacher has only to pause in his
moralizing and say something like, 'One day I met my next
door neighbour in his greenhouse . . .' and bored eyes look
up from idle perusal of A Table to Find Easter in the Prayer
Book, minds which had drifted far return to the scene and
the substance. But why are stories of greater interest than
moral lectures and other kinds of discursive talk? No
doubt part of the answer is that stories feature people and
events, recognizable happenings; but the main reason why
we like stories is because they do not – or at least they

should not – drive a moral lesson too far. An ethical proposition may tell us just how much good we ought to do and how we should go about doing it. A story, because it is a work of imagination, leaves something to the reader's imagination.

Take that parable of the Good Samaritan again. Perhaps Jesus could have decided never to tell it but, instead, to issue some general rule about the demands of charity transcending racial boundaries. That is what most preachers do with that parable, and so ruin it. But we can argue with the preacher. We can even argue with those parts of religious teaching which are discursive and pre-scriptive – like the food laws of ancient Israel or St Paul's strictness on what women should or should not be allowed to do in church, or even with the Ten Commandments. But it is impossible to argue with a story, except by telling a different story.

The interpreter who claims that the Good Samaritan is 'really about' the transcending power of charity over racial differences is making one point about the story, and there is no guarantee that his point is the same as the one originally intended by the storyteller. Perhaps the story was meant to demonstrate the hypocrisy of the priest, the shallow spirituality of the Levite, or even the innocent trust of the innkeeper who was prepared to wait for the Samaritan to return before being paid the bill? True, Jesus did add an epilogue to this parable in the form of a question: 'Who was the neighbour to him that fell among thieves? . . . Go and do thou likewise.' But there is no precise formulation to how we are to 'do likewise'. And it should be remembered that the telling of the parable originated out of a demand for clarification of the term 'neighbour'. We may ask if it was successful in answering that question.

The New Testament scholar Joachim Jeremias became famous for his insistence that the parables of Jesus were usually intended to have one meaning and one meaning only. But if this were true, it would have been quicker and certainly less confusing to the audience for the one meaning to have been given in the form of a moral precept in each case. I think they are examples of irony, vagueness and systematic ambiguity. Many different meanings and allusions can be teased out of the parables: they can be read as concretized versions of the ethical teaching given in the Sermon on the Mount; as contrasts between the morality of this-worldliness and the ethics of the Kingdom of God; or as spiritual meditations which characterize the warring factions within every human personality. This last method of interpretation is particularly rich from a psychological point of view as we discover that there is something of the Prodigal, the Elder Brother and the Unjust Steward as well as the Forgiving Father and The Good Samaritan in each one of us; those characters can be seen as standing for singular aspects of ourself which is not singular but made up of many contradictory parts. Thus the resolution of the parable, its end, can offer guidance on how the individual personality may achieve its end or final purpose, its *telos* and integration. That was one reason for telling the stories in the first place: that they might bring salvation to their hearers and readers.

But parables are more than their meanings. If parables were simply ways of getting across a literal, non-parabolic message then the language and value of the parables remain of only secondary importance: they become subordinate to the message or the meaning. Whereas, the parable is its own meaning. And this meaning is the actual words of the particular parable. In living languages there are no complete synonyms and it is impossible to render the meaning of any word exactly and entirely by means of another word. This is because words do not only *refer* (denote objects and persons, actions and so on), but they *connote*, which is to say that they have associations and connections which, though not part of the immediate denotation or reference, are inescapable. For example, 'harlot' and 'prostitute' denote the same occupation: but with the first we are perhaps led to biblical and Shakespearian courtesans; while the second tends to conjure up visions of low life in modern industrial cities. Even words as nondescript and functional as 'a' and 'an' produce different associations – nouns which either begin or do not begin with a vowel. The exact words used in any parable continue to make up its meaning; and we approach the fullness of the meaning when we are fully acquainted with the words in their proper order. 'Fell among thieves' indicates a milieu widely different from 'was set upon by bandits'. The resonances of 'thieves' include, even confining ourselves to the words of Scripture, the thieves on Calvary and perhaps the expression 'as a thief in the night'. But with 'bandits' we enter another world entirely: the celluloid and popcorn world of El Dorado and the Saturday matinée.

Our grandparents knew that meanings are located in the precise order of particular words in a given story. That is why so much importance was attached to repetition, learning by heart and reading, marking, learning, inwardly digesting. Interesting, if depressing, to note that the modern world has no use for 'by heart' and has even replaced that phrase by the pejorative, mechanical 'by rote'. We learn the meaning of a parable not by definitions, extrapolations and explanations but by entering its own imaginative world. We are bored by the slogans and catchphrases of moral exhortation but we can return again and again to a good story – and the parables are certainly that – and discover new depths in it. We do not translate or abstract meaning; we *approach* it. And a powerful story is holy ground. We must do the literary equivalent of taking off our shoes: this means adopting a certain humility before the text, not attempting to analyse it in any way which is external to the words themselves. When we say that a text is inspired we mean precisely that its words possess a numinous, holy quality. It strikes me as very odd that those Christians who make so much of the Spirit and of inspiration are usually the same people who think that any old version – usually *new* version! – of the Bible will do. This makes the parable into a sort of vague essence which hovers over numberless expressions of itself: AV, Jerusalem Bible, NEB, Good News and so on to fill a whole page with the mere titles of the versions now available. In the light of what has been said about the absence of true synonyms, of reference and connotation, it provokes the question of how a common religious sensibility can be said to exist any longer when the one thing needful for this – a common text, preferably known by heart – is not available. The choice of text is not a trivial matter. It must, in order to be an effective vehicle for religion, be one that is known to succeeding generations, or else we lose continuity with both past and future and the experience referred to as 'religious' becomes ephemeral – which is to say not religious at all, but secular. Texts create communities and whole cultures. Each civilization produces its epics near its beginning. Words do possess numinous power and this power is intensified by time and use. That is what Eliot said, better, in his expression, 'The communication of the dead is tongued with fire beyond the language of the living.' Sacred texts are like sacred buildings: they are hallowed by the repeated visits and valid prayers of succeeding generations. The only English texts which, even at this late stage, could begin to produce a common religious sensibility are the Authorised Version of the Bible and the Book of Common Prayer. Even in our present cultural attenuation, these books are the only religious texts which still produce echoes in non-literary communication. These echoes – of the Lord's Prayer, of phrases like 'stony ground', and 'fatted calf' – are fading fast, though it is surprising to see how often they are still used in the news and features columns of the daily papers. When you hear miners' pickets jeering at those who cross their lines not with the word 'traitor' but with 'Judas', you learn something about the way in which religious communality is maintained. What chance is there of religious sensibility of any kind when the new eucharistic rites include four, optional, alternative forms of what used to be the one Prayer of Consecration and, worse, when there are half a dozen versions of the Lord's Prayer on offer? Anyone who has ever tried to teach children knows how difficult this is even when what you want to teach is single, simple, undivided and supported by a wide acquaintance and use in the community. How to teach Scripture, how to inculcate by repetition, suggestion and allusion the sense of the mystery of a sacred text in our present Babel of alternative versions is a question I would not like to have to answer. And yet, it is a question which faces anyone who still has a concern for religious English. Of one thing we can be sure: no one will learn the new texts by heart, or even by rote. They are not memorable so they will not be remembered.

The parables of Jesus themselves reveal something of Christianity's particular form: they are a putting into flesh, an incarnation in fictional characters, of the mind and Spirit of Christ. When we hear or read the parables, we do much more than learn to acknowledge moral or spiritual truths in the abstract; in fact Christianity knows nothing of such truths but is always concerned with real life, with incarnation. Deep in a shared cultural and spiritual life and language, those characters from the parables live. They may be regarded as standing for archetypes, but each character is more than a type. He is a person. How well, for example, we feel we know the two brothers in the Prodigal Son. To ask whether the parable is true produces the answer that it is real, because the characters are real human beings full of a life and personality of their own. The Christian doctrine of incarnation means that the highest values in human life are to be found in actual human beings. Apply that doctrine to the language of faith, and we see that the highest expression of those same values occurs in the creation of characters and story. The stories have saving power because we are able to enter them in a way not available in discursive prose or ethical prescriptions. We are led through identification with the humanity – graces and faults alike – of the characters and the realism of the fictional world to experience in ourselves the emotions and moral conflicts of recognizable human beings. We become by turns Priest, Levite and Samaritan in the story of the man who fell among thieves. We experience the remorse of the Prodigal because by reading that parable we *become* him, just as we become the Elder Brother and the Merciful Father. It makes no sense to ask of these saving stories whether, as a matter of fact, they are true: nothing could be truer.

Now, if this is true of the parables, it is also true of the story of Jesus himself. To say that Jesus is God incarnate may be to claim that he came from the eternal unseen world of heaven and lived as a man the life of this world. But that particular way of construing the incarnation is only one way among many. It is not itself the incarnation but only the incarnation explained according to the rules of a particular metaphysical system: the system of the invisible, eternal world which is alleged to exist behind or beyond this world. Some men at some time in history will find this particular way of understanding the incarnation more vivid and valuable than other men will find it at other times. Incarnation itself as a doctrine is not a literal truth. What *could* the literal truth ever be? How could it be stated? 'He came down to earth from heaven' is obviously a pictorial gesture involving metaphors of space and movement of two distinct *places*. Similarly, the much more philosophical language of 'The Word which had for ever pre-existed with the Father became flesh' is a metaphor.

The logical grammar of the sentence means it must be a metaphor, since no meaning of a literal kind can be given to it. 'Word' and 'Father' are technical theological terms which have only a loose connection with the way in which these terms are ordinarily used. Conceptual confusion is bound to result when we insist on taking literally that which by its nature cannot possibly have been meant as a literal statement of fact.

It is vital to clear up this conceptual confusion, for nonsense remains nonsense even when it is made to sound like holy nonsense. Books, heretics and wars of religion have arisen repeatedly out of someone's belief that what was being affirmed, denied or challenged was a precise theological statement when nothing of the kind was at issue. *The Myth of God Incarnate* was a case in point. What did those critical essayists imagine they were denying? And what, in their equally strident but equally confused reply, *The Truth of God Incarnate*, did conservative theologians imagine they were affirming? Attack and defence alike depended on the propensity to regard metaphors as literal truths. The incarnation may be described in the words of Mrs C. F. Alexander's hymn, or it may be adduced and argued about in the terminology of the fourth-century Fathers or the Schoolmen, or even in that of *Lux Mundi* or Eduard Schillebeeckx. But it may also be represented by a Madonna and child or by the music of *Et Incarnatus Est* from Mozart's C Minor Mass. And in these latter cases, the force of propositional truth is weak or absent altogether; yet something is being affirmed, though not in a form which can be *literally* denied. Much the same as can be said about the superiority of stories to discursive prose can also be said about the superiority of masterpieces of painting and music to the bare form of theological proposition. It is only the paucity of imagination which makes us hanker after the formula, the letter of truth. In fact, literal language will only ever take us as far as the truths of science and we have seen how those are not sufficient to sustain the fullness of human life and experience. For almost *all* our language is metaphorical even when we think we are speaking the purest literalisms: we talk of 'sunrise' (but after Copernicus?); of the stars 'coming out' and so on. A good party game: see who can talk for the longest stretch without lapsing into metaphorical usage!

So to the biblically reported events of Jesus' life. These are in themselves the most powerful statement of the incarnation. If we want to know what 'incarnation' means, we should simply read the gospel story. What doctrine or mere theory could give us a better understanding? The ordinary novelist or storyteller creates a world, offers it to his readers and says, in effect, 'The world is really like this, isn't it?' And the job of the literary critic as well as the general reader is to evaluate, taste and see, whether the novelist's vision is compelling. The power of the gospel story is infinitely great because, dealing with the theme of what is infinite, it convinces us that whatever may be meant by doctrines of incarnation, this is in truth what it really looks like. *This* is the Son of God? Yes. In so far as we may use such strange and confusing terms, if God were to be incarnate and live among men, *this* is what it would be like? Yes. The stories themselves are the putting into flesh of abstract theological principles. There follows a conclusion of revolutionary proportions for preacher and hearer alike: the stories about Jesus must never be invoked in order to express or support a moral or spiritual opinion which is alleged to be *the meaning* of Christianity – usually these morals and opinions are held as it were *a priori* and independently of the text, and the words of the text are often crudely dragged in so that 'authority' may be lent to the preacher's views. The whole practice of discovering moral and spiritual guidance in the gospel story must consist of the closest attention to the particular events there described. Meditation on those events, reading, marking, learning and inwardly digesting until the story becomes a part of us.

To ask, therefore, whether the story of Jesus is true is not to ask whether this or that event took place in Capernaum or Nazareth or wherever it may have been. It is to ask, 'Is this story telling us the fullest truth about what it is to be a man in this world?' And that is the same as asking whether the story is a true incarnation. Of course, other answers may be given to final questions of this sort. The particular answers given represent the several great religions of the world. No single story, metaphor or picture is true for all times and places. And yet the various stories are not always necessarily contradictory. In what way can a picture be said to contradict another picture? Religion is cultural. That is to say it belongs to specific people in specific times and locations. It is meaningless to ask whether the Judaism of Jeremiah at the time of the exile is more true – as if on some eternal scale of spiritual values – than, say, the Christianity of St Paul. There is no highway to eternal scales of values outside a particular culture. A culture too is an incarnation of life and values. There is no extra-cultural access to transcendent ideals. The connection with language is again prominent: it was Simone Weil who said that equal dangers exist in a writer changing his language and a man changing his religion. It can be done, of course, but to change one's language is to change everything, the whole system of perceiving the world, for language is what creates our world; and the world of a Russian speaker is necessarily a different place from that of one who speaks English as his native tongue. Religion as story incarnates our spirituality. So, if we change the story by converting to, say, Islam, we change the spirituality. Needless to say, everything else would be changed as well including our relationship with society, the pattern of family life, even diet, dress and daily timetable. Culture is not only the clothes or adornment of thought; it is thought's limbs and sinews. Although there are different cultures, one's own culture is absolute because it is one's whole life, limits and boundaries, one's incarnation.

Culture is the means by which a commentary on the basic story is continued. And the best commentaries are themselves imaginative works, stories, paintings and musical compositions. The spiritual strength of a culture, then, is to be measured by the creative power and insights of its imaginative works, its art. For it is art, within a culture and therefore always referring back explicitly or implicitly to the sacred text of that culture, which in each succeeding generation holds up that picture of experience and asks us to agree that life is like *this*.

For a thousand years in England culture was shaped by a version of the Christian faith administered by institutionalized authority. In the age when great cathedrals were built, organization in this world, feudalism, was paralleled by the theologians' metaphysical picture of heaven. Grades of angels were eternal types of the grades of men. Politics and theology were thus bound together in one system and it was the power of that system and the singleness of its vision which provided the conditions for such a sustained period of high cultural achievement. It was the age of Chartres and York Minster, of Anselm and Aquinas, of musical form as the parallel of architectural style – antiphonal plainchant and the symmetry of the gothic arch, hierarchical, God at the high central point surveying all the activities of angels and men; the whole summed up in Dante's *Divine Comedy*.

It is foolish to look for complete unanimity of belief in any age, but the Middle Ages were the period when Christian society enjoyed more homogeneity of will and purpose than at any other time before or since. Of course, it was no perfect world. There was plague, poverty, superstition, the hounding of women in the witch hunts, and the wars of religion. But no one who has read Augustine will waste his time looking for the perfection of heaven in the kingdoms of this world. The Middle Ages provided a cultural expression of Christianity which nurtured and sustained society, giving to individual men and women points of reference, a scheme of salvation; if I may so put it, a beginning, a middle and an end. Medieval Christianity told a coherent story. And, for all the logic-chopping of the Schoolmen, it was a remarkably vivid story of redemption after the Fall, of life out of death; and it was told gloriously in the music, painting and architecture of the period. If we in our automated cities, among all our concrete and glass, still regard the ancient cathedrals as infinitely more solid, more assured, than anything we have produced, imagine what emblems of the eternal kingdom they must have appeared to the medieval peasant from his own primitive dwelling. To live in England in the Middle Ages was to be given a blik, an outlook, that was imposed with political authority, enshrined in daily practice, envisaged and portrayed by artists and logically defended by the scholars. An imperfect world, no doubt; but a world which told a story to which the people belonged.

But history moves all, and, for a great complexity of reasons (trade, the crusades, European wars and the rise of nationalism, the discovery of the American continent and new currents in humanistic and scientific ideas), the medieval vision was fragmented. It is no use our bemoaning the fact. We cannot 'summon the spectre of a rose or follow an antique drum'. All cravings for a romanticized past, the golden age, are only nostalgia – a thought that may one day dawn in the minds of our contemporary revivalists who imagine that it is both possible and desirable to live the lives of first-century Corinthian Christians in today's bedsitland and suburbia. The fragmenting of the medieval vision was not an unmitigated cultural catastrophe, for there was creative energy in the very activities which caused the split. The Middle Ages represented the perfectibility of man in the image of the completely faithful and obedient God-man, Jesus Christ. In much of this representation, Christ is scarcely human at all – though the paintings of the Passion and Crucifixion by Giotto are a powerful counterbalance. So the gap between idealized man and man as he actually experienced himself becomes too great, the psychological burden, guilt, too much to bear. Shakespeare, the genius of his time and language, aware of cultural antecedents, tradition, gives us out of this disjunction another sort of man, a man who is more like us: Hamlet. A Christian prince but not of the idealized medieval sort. One given to doubt and anxiety, strange dreams and the 'antic disposition'. Contemplating suicide. Not looking forward in faith and hope to the life of the world to come, but afraid of the prospect – 'To sleep, perchance to dream. Aye, there's the rub.' The prize of eternal life, the great consolation to medieval man, becomes a curse to the new sort of man symbolized and represented by Hamlet. But no one says Shakespeare's play is a blasphemous fable. It is a sincere drama, a true story, because when we look at the demented protagonist filled with doubt and foreboding we recognize a big part of ourselves. And it is this new experience that faith must speak to, whose spirituality must be acknowledged, whch must also become part of our story.

The movement from faith to doubt occurs in another formative thinker of the Renaissance, René Descartes. Anselm began with faith seeking understanding (*Fides Quaerens Intellectum*); Descartes began with systematic doubt and the *via negativa* of 'I doubt therefore I think'. And in Descartes there is another great cultural shift – from incarnation to conceptualization. For medieval man the world was solid, tangible, incarnation; the cathedrals, indubitable combinations of spirit and flesh. In Descartes, mental events are what is most real. Men of the ability of

Shakespeare and Descartes do not simply invent their plays or their philosophy in a vacuum; they are acutely sensitive to the language and thought of their time; at home in their cultural traditions. They respond to the influences of the age and, by means of great artistic or philosophical power, redirect the living culture: that is, they add to the story and so retell it. To do that you have to be a man of quite extraordinary sensitivity, to assimilate and recreate the story of your time: in a word, you have to be a prophet.

The story of western culture from the time of Shakespeare and Descartes to our own is one of increasing fragmentation. The unity of the medieval vision is shattered again and again. Still, the cultural story is told, unravels itself, from the standpoint of the biblical text. There is no escape from our institutionalized Christian past. Salvation is still a key concept but in such as Luther and the later protestant evangelists, it is not salvation of the race or the Church any longer but *my* salvation brought about by *my* penitence for *my* sins. One can easily imagine Luther's message to Hamlet. The individual and his feelings become ever more important in Luther who needed to feel the assurance of God's forgiveness, in Wesley whose heart, as he tells us, 'was strangely warmed' in that old Moravian chapel. Religion becomes individual and intense. Romanticism rules. Christ meets Faust. It is a cultural story which arrives at symptoms of self-parody in the productions of the pre-Raphaelites and A. C. Swinburne.

We must live with our contemporary story. There is no living possibility of our doing anything else. We cannot re-invent baroque or classical culture. We may not return to the ecclesiastical spiritual settlement of the sixteenth century any more than we can return to the Middle Ages, to the faith of the early Church or to the theocratic ideal of ancient Israel. It is in the here and now, in our living story, that we must create our spirituality however unpropitious the conditions may seem. Just how unpropitious can be indicated by the mention of some of the most recent and revolutionary influences in our culture. Science, which already regarded man as molecules and plasma, made not in the image of God but in that of the ape, defines us with ever greater impersonalization and soullessness in the work of writers like B. F. Skinner and the behavioural psychologists. These new Schoolmen not only deny the existence of soul and mind, but they eliminate all traces of character and personality from what they refer to as 'the organism', which is only a bundle of stimuli and responses whose behaviour can be endlessly modified and controlled by 'operant conditioning'. As Arthur Koestler once said, 'Now that man has lost his soul, gone out of his mind and seems to be about to lose all consciousness, what is there left for the psychologist to study? Professor Skinner's answer is, Rats.' And in the early work of Freud the encouraging part of our story which said we are made in the image of God is replaced by the notion that even our finest achievements and most unselfish acts are only instances of sexual sublimation. (A new connotation for the word 'sublime' there!) God is totem and taboo.

Our culture seems to be an exact reversal of the medieval system. All is fragmented. The individual, not the Church or the state, is of greatest significance. We are not welded into a common body but thrown apart into inescapable isolation. And over this isolation broods no Spirit of God, only prophecies of meaninglessness and death. Ours is the culture of *The Waste Land*, of Dante's arena of despair: 'So many, I had not thought death had undone so many'. Our philosophers tell us that to claim 'God exists' is grammatically senseless, syntactically impossible, that it is no use trying to reason about morality. The Poet Laureate preaches nature red in tooth and claw, rabid evolutionism. The great modernist writers returned to the Heracleitan flux without meaning in the technique called 'stream of consciousness'. Even in the 1920s Eliot could see that we are 'hollow men, head piece filled with straw' and that there are no 'roots that clutch' no 'branches grow out of this stony rubbish' as we 'know only a heap of broken images'. The discarnation continues via theoretical physics in which matter is reduced to equations, abstract painting which has abandoned the human form divine, and music serial and electronic. The exquisite crucifixion which was the late romanticism of Wagner, Mahler, Strindberg, pre-Raphaelitism, Symbolism and Decadence has given way to a shadowy afterlife which is banal and absurd, where Samuel Beckett's tramps grub around in wastebins in order to find 'something so revolting that they might be put off eating for ever'.

Circumstances which are far from propitious. And yet this is our culture, our story, and if spirituality is to be created at all, it must be created out of this. Clutching roots must be found or, alternatively, we must learn to live with rootlessness. In the nineteenth century, Thomas Carlyle said the whole world is a wilderness in an atheistic century. Nietzsche captured the feeling of loneliness and emptiness in the solemn pronouncement, 'God is dead'. A hundred years later we have come so far into that wilderness as to have lost our hold of language about God; categories such as 'theist', 'atheist' and 'agnostic' are largely meaningless; and the Church itself is reduced to a quaint sect, a movement among movements, divided into twin irrelevancies of secularizers and literal-minded enthusiasts for so-called 'New Testament Christianity'. There is no more depressing task for the contemporary clergyman than to officiate at rites of passage for the unchurched: it is as if they come, awkward and embarrassed, but hoping that some meaning and significance will be provided by the priest and by the rite. But the cultural links have been broken and the story is too long to tell at a baptism, wedding or funeral. The roots of religious consciousness no longer clutch. And yet, if people could still be genuinely stirred by historic Christian faith and practice, it would surely be at times like these.

The cultural climate is one of meaninglessness, inconsequentiality; there is a widespread look of negative aggressiveness: 'So what?' It is as if the cat has been let out of the bag. Religion has been shown to be bunk – by science. The king has no clothes. God is dead. The mood is apathy. Beckett's tramps acting out our lives gratuitously because we must do something while we are here. And, often, thought does not even proceed as far as the point of apathy as people lose themselves in pursuit of goals which they are told are desirable by a cynical advertisement industry and a cavalcade of 'consumer' programmes based on the crudest version of 'maximize pleasure and minimize pain'. This is the hell of Aldous Huxley's *Brave New World* in which the damned do not, cannot, even reflect on their predicament, but live out their lives as automata. The nursery rhymes have been replaced by commercial jingles on television in the new folk-religion of pop-materialism. How prophetic was Huxley's own jingle: 'Streptocock-Gee to Banbury T, to see a fine bathroom and WC.' And a university place for my children please: a 2-1 in classics will lead to a good job with the private television company 'marketing' 'documentary units' for 'the network'. Yes, there is a net and we are all caught in it.

Here I want to try to say something to the person who is not so utterly beguiled by the mass-media and the sales talk of the epoch, to the person who knows that we are living in the age of the wasteland, of hollow men and the Absurd. What is to be done?

Medieval Christianity was a wonderful system but open to many imperfections and abuses. Every culture has its dark side. Our culture is different in that it turns *first* its dark side to us, and the spiritual achievements of the age are difficult to discover and identify. But if we live in the time after the death of God, we ought to see that we are bequeathed an enormous freedom. The apprehension of this freedom, when it dawns on us emotionally as well as intellectually, is itself a religious experience. Suppose we are as free as Nietzsche said we were! Our wills sovereign in a godless universe. That must make any reflective man fear and tremble and ask, as Nietzsche himself asked, 'Not free *from* what but free *for* what?' In other words, there is a sense in which, if there is no God, mankind has more responsibility, not less. Besides, no culture, not even our own, is without precedent. Deeply spiritual men in the past have felt awful isolation and purposelessness deriving from the absence of God. The right course of action in such circumstances was always thought to be to accept and take deeply into oneself the sense of meaninglessness, to express it as a genuine spiritual experience and to wait patiently for God's return. One of our problems is that our age is so secularized and scientifically orientated that we are too proud or too careless to imagine that anyone else experienced our predicament before, say, 1872 – an apt choice of year, the birthday of that great utilitarian Bertrand Russell.

We do not really believe that the psalmist's despair, when he cried out to the absent God, was as serious as ours. But do we think he was acting, insincere? Poetry of that order – of an order which this enlightened age finds difficult to emulate – does not grow out of insincerity of feeling! The psalmist was prepared to proclaim his bereftness. It might help us if we were to do the same instead of turning a subjective statement of loss into an objective statement of negative ontology: There is no God. That is what Beckett does, and there is a sense in which the trilogy of novels and the later minimalist writing are like one long psalm of complaint. And yet those works of fiction point to, and indeed themselves embody, a great spiritual truth: you may proclaim the death of God, but it changes nothing; all the old human and religious feelings and dispositions are still with us. Beckett has provided a spirituality of the void.

When we read *Molloy*, we do not enter a world of mechanism, of scientism and soulless technology. We do enter a world which is macabre and sinister but it is a world of human feeling, even the affirmation of loss: 'I cannot go on. I must go on. I will go on'. The triumph of the human spirit over the metaphysics of despair. It does not matter that the particular human spirit happens to reside in a tramp, an unrespectable man, an outsider. The prophets were hardly respectable. Jesus was an outsider, and crucified outside the city wall. By encapsulating our predicament in his fiction, Beckett overcomes the fear of meaninglessness; and he does this most successfully by a transcending humour. Those tramps have saving and redeeming wit; not belly laughs as in Rabelais, or poking fun at others, but a genuinely self-transcending humour that gives a sense of perspective which, in an older spiritual vocabulary, was given by more sombre figures. The same is true in the doctrine of Absurdity in the work of Albert Camus: a sense of the absurdity of things provides a sense of freedom which is numinous and powerfully creative.

The novels of Beckett, the music of Alban Berg, the early poetry of T. S. Eliot leave no one in any doubt that human creativity can triumph over the void, rise above it, demonstrate superiority to it by defining it artistically. And that is the same task which faced the psalmist. It is bringing forth a new language of spirituality, a task requiring immense forces of intelligence, emotional power and – word beloved of the mystics – 'concentration'. It resembles the labour of hewing stones and striking water from the stony rock.

> 'April is the cruellest month
> Breeding lilacs out of the dead land . . .'

It is as good as, 'We have walked in stony places, O Lord, and found thee absent'.

Our fictional heroes are secularized versions of our

Christ image. This is necessarily so, since the figure of Christ predominates in the literature of western civilization. At the high point of Christian culture the hero was a prince possessing material wealth and spiritual power; in the great English novels of the last century he was embodied in a variety of characters from the noble craftsman Adam Bede to the intellectual Daniel Deronda. In modern fiction the heroes are nonentities, displaced persons and tramps. One big difference between the heroes of past convention and those of our period is that the modern hero, as tramp, is not so governed by order, routine and clock time. Heroes from earlier periods developed their character within a framework of duties and obligations, according to a schedule of conventional relationships — hence the introduction of unconventionality as a device causing shock — within a world of meaning. Beckett's heroes, like Camus' heroes, live outside ordered society and even outside the romantic alternative to the bourgeois world which was inhabited by characters like Heathcliff and Jude the Obscure. The tramps are amoral, not out of wilfulness but out of bewilderment. They do not perform either the bourgeois duty or the romantic gesture. A typical attitude in Beckett towards love and sex, deliberately mocking the romantic hero's exquisite shocks of passion, is to be found in *Molloy*:

> . . . when she, undertaking me from behind, thrust her stick between my legs and began to titillate my privates. She gave me money after each session, to me who would have consented to know love and probe it to the bottom, without charge. But she was an idealist. I would have preferred it seems to me an orifice less arid and roomy, that would have given me a higher opinion of love, it seems to me.

Beckett's tramps are outside society, outside a realm of order which bestows meaning on daily life. But, because there is only one world, even these outsiders are obliged to make contact with it from time to time. When they do so, as outsiders, they perform in ways which are inconsistent with the order into which they have intruded themselves — often hilariously. They are perplexed opportunists, taking what they need, taking what they can from a world which would rather ignore them. They forage and find a scrap here and a scrap there and then go on their way. It seems to me that this too is an image of the sort of spiritual life which is available in this era of absurdity: no rich diet but a piece of sustenance here and there, only half expected in forms which are surprising. Accidental graces.

Paradoxically, the stateless tramps in Beckett's novels share an attitude which was met with usually and only in connection with religious people, and with high calibre religious at that — saints, monks, spiritual directors and the like. They contemplate. We too, as readers living in the time of the Absurd, are free to contemplate; indeed, faced with a world that is incomprehensible, because all systems of explanation are absurd, contemplation of the flux of events becomes a necessity. Minds must do *something*. And the old formal method of contemplation is strangely suitable for use in a world without meaning, for the traditional directors always said that the highest form of prayer is achieved only by stripping the mind of all thought and reason, all images and accustomed connections. That is precisely the condition which meaninglessness thrusts upon us. In my opinion, the logic and form of the Absurd is finally the same as that of traditional spirituality. By emptying ourselves we are filled. By going into the desert places we become fruitful. By renunciation we find we have received all. Come then, take out *The Waste Land* with more cheerfulness than usual!

The modern culture that I have been writing about is, of course, modernist culture — that revolutionary movement which was, in a variety of styles, represented by Eliot,

Pound, Wyndham Lewis, Picasso, Braque and the musicians of the Second Viennese School – Schoenberg, Berg and Webern. That movement changed everything in art and its influence cannot be escaped even sixty or seventy years later. Modernism *is* our culture. And yet there have been, and continue to be new developments as artists and writers move away from minimalism, the world of small forms and all the self-conscious building of artificial systems of order such as serial composition or Stravinsky's strict bitonality, or his even stricter neo-classicalism. These developments are very recent and therefore they are the most difficult to understand. I wonder if it is too early to say that there is a movement from what is gratuitous to a new order of purposefulness?

I think a post-modern movement on these lines can be detected in the work of some of our leading exponents. It is as if they have grubbed around in the waste land until they have discovered small places which, though not full of luxurious fruits, at least look as if they might one day bear fruit. The composer Edward Cowie was, until the mid-1970s, a serial composer of enormous accomplishment. His scores (e.g. *Leviathan*) were dense models of mathematical relationships. But towards the end of another work composed at the same time (*Gesangbuch*) there appears the hint and echo of traditional tonality. Even Stockhausen – though one vulture does not always indicate a carcase – has spent seventy minutes of a recent piece in G major. Post-modern novels – *Christopher Homm* by C. H. Sisson for instance – often seem to be trying to eschew artifice and demonstrate a simplicity which is not the same as nineteenth-century realism but that realism purified by the modernist shock. The critic Martin Seymour-Smith claims that Sisson has 'surpassed Beckett'. Well, that may be. He has certainly acknowledged an aspect of his hero's being which is not made explicit in any of Beckett's tramps: the 'Christ of a Man' (Homm) who is nevertheless, in his way, every bit as much of an outsider and an outcast as Beckett's wretches. What are we to make of the reappearance of recognizable human figures in some very recent paintings?

One of the most far-reaching results of the Absurd, and of modernism, is the production of radical individuality. In Mozart's time everyone who wrote music in Europe wrote music that was recognizably similar to everyone else's. It is not always easy to tell Mozart from Haydn and much harder to differentiate among slightly less well-known composers such as Cherubini and Hummel, Attwood, Stamitz and J. C. Bach. In our own age, artists display a much wider range of style and method: among composers, for instance, there are worlds of difference between Peter Maxwell Davies and Alois Zimmerman, between Karlheinz Stockhausen and Robert Simpson. Are we to conclude, then, that the single story of culture has become fragmented and dissipated to such an extent that it no longer exists except in a confusing plethora of individual stories – every man his own prophet, every man his own God? Perhaps.

Certainly there are numerous styles of spirituality from food fads (just like the ancient gnostics!) to personal gurus, from the joy through strength cultivation of the body to the so called 'fringe religions'. There is also a widespread longing for a kind of companionship and all-togetherness – 'members of one body' – which cannot be supplied by anything other than a national, European or Western culture. Sporadic outbreaks of fellow feeling such as the charismatic movement in the official churches and in house groups will never produce genuine cultural renewal because they are shallow, banal. Their banality derives from their misguided programme of trying to restore a cultural epoch (or selected parts of it) which has long since disappeared. As Sisson says in another context, to do that sort of thing is to produce only what is 'sham-antique'. Other opportunities for the rediscovery of our spiritual story, or rather for the retelling of our spiritual story, may exist in the psychological ideas of C. G. Jung. His psychological-spiritual programme which aims at 'individuation' of the personality is a detailed working out of the meaning of the phrase, 'The Kingdom of God is within you'. This amounts first to an extremely individualistic exercise, exploring one's own psyche – contemplating one's own navel as the detractors say; but, because this exercise culminates in the discovery that we all contain, or are possessed by, the same archetypal figures – Shadow, Anima, Selbst – it may be said to point to a new and future communality. There is much that is helpful and revealing in what Jung had to say but his work is terribly bowdlerized and trendified by well-heeled pseudo mystics from the gin and kaftan belt. I have said all I can say about Jung and spirituality in my book *Being Saved*.

Our future spirituality, like all earlier spiritualities, will be conditioned by historical developments; and, as ever, it will itself help to produce those developments – some of which may be a time of tribulation so terrible that, unless the days be shortened, no one will be able to bear it. I shall try to say something about this in a later chapter on Apocalypse and Wisdom. For the present, it seems to me that we have no alternative but to enter as deeply and as seriously as we can into the perplexities which afflict our time. The land is waste and the sky is dark. But there are luminaries who bring life even out of dead places by encapsulating and transcending those places in their creative work. Our creative, spiritual work is to listen to the prophets of our own time.

5
The New Sectarianism and the End of the World

The collapse of a unifying tradition means that we live in an age of rampant sectarianism, of hundreds of different and competing solutions to our spiritual problems. There are the many Christian denominations, mainstream, authoritative and coherent; but there are also the newer and more informal groupings, like the growing House Church movement, in which rigour and consistency in theological formulation are rare. Orthodoxy is transmuted by whim. Individuals acting on their own authority and enthusiasm claim to make inspired pronouncements which soon become binding on the group – until some other, 'newer' pronouncement is made. The exercise of religion becomes a matter of changing fashion.

It is usually felt necessary to find some sort of backing for modish spuriousness, so the sectarian leader does not stand up and say, in effect, 'Look at me: guess what I've just invented!' Instead, he talks piously about the 'rediscovery' of some ancient and vital Christian experience which has been neglected by tradition. If the experience can be traced back as far as New Testament times, so much the better: then Corinth lives again in Ruislip as the group believes itself to be a congregation of the saved set in a naughty world. Selective fundamentalism. A faith and practice which is sham antique, summoning the spectre of a rose. The experience belongs neither wholly in St Paul's time nor wholly in our own. Rootless and eclectic, the moral manifestation is sentimentalism. The substance of sectarianism repeats itself in a rota of banality and what is 'new' has been before: adventism, revivalism, muscular Christianity, moral rearmament, speaking in tongues, healings, exorcism and so on through a very long list, aspects of religion which are by turns exalted to become the essence of religion. No pope was ever more infallible than the enthusiast for revival.

All this has happened before in the history of the early Church among the Gnostic sects. The Marcionites and Libertarians who contrasted the Just God with the Good God; the Arians who denied the eternal sonship of Christ; the Valentinians who posited creation by the Demiurge; the Docetists who denied Christ's actual sufferings. These sects have returned in our own time, albeit often in re-mythologized forms. Even our errors are cast in the language and thought of the age. Irenaeus tilted against the Adventists and those who believed in the efficacy of diet and secret doctrine; is it only mischievous to imagine that, were he to appear in our day, he would find himself in contention with CND and the apologists for 'health foods'?

The Gnostics claimed to know a secret truth which could redeem man from the miseries of the world. Since T. H. Huxley's famous remark, we have lived in an agnostic civilization, but one littered with new manifestations of the Gnostics' secret doctrine. There are the so called 'fringe religions' and the cults, all of them promising the excitement of exclusivity and the comfort of togetherness and, incidentally, the secret doctrine that alone can bring man peace and happiness. So many contradictory versions of absolute truth: Guru Bhagwan, Divine Light, Children of God, Moonies and so on. Beyond these are the semi-secular therapies: the higher wisdom of jogging; the attempt to prove that man lives by bread alone so long as it is wholemeal; the avid encounter groups; the gasping addicts of aerobics – is it an unconscious attempt to imbibe some spirit (*pneuma* = air or spirit)? There are the Jung folks, up to their armpits in anima, relentlessly avowing the importance of being individuated. Exotic imports flourish on the right side of town: T'ai Chi, Acupuncture, I Ching, Tantric Meditation, Zen. All these movements claim to offer the key to happiness and although some of them are tinged with a sort of pseudo-science – a recent programme on BBC television spoke of 'the scientific way to fulfilment' – they have arisen at least partly in protest against the claim of science to have the measure of man.

For the salvation offered by science is mechanical, general and impersonal. Since we are bundles of drives driven by smaller bundles of molecules, our frustrations and gratifications can be quantified and then, in theory at least, abolished or provided for. The official scientific Gnosis of our age is Behavioural Psychology. Like ancient Gnosticism it has its secret doctrine and private language. The human being is 'the organism'; feelings are 'affective states'; happenings in the world around us are 'unconditioned stimuli'; intention, will and action merge into the summary expression 'conditioned reflex' – since any suggestion that there is actually someone doing the intending, willing or acting is to believe the false doctrine of the Ghost in the Machine.

The behaviourist believes – *with what faculty?* – that man is a machine. There follows the scientific exorcism: no ghosts in the machine. The whole system is an attempt to talk about human beings as if we were aspects of technology, to describe our nature in 'objective', scientifically measureable terms. The progress of behaviourism follows dutifully that of scientific mechanism and, with the coming of the computer, there is much talk of the organism in the language of Information Theory. Of course, it is possible to talk about human beings in this way, but our humanity will resist all such talk and, despite the superior wisdom of organisms like Professor Skinner, we shall continue to insist that our inner world of desires and intentions is real, that it is no mere ghost which loves, fears, anguishes, repents or falls in love. Behaviourism may indeed describe the organism but it says nothing about human beings. In any case, its claims are contradictory since even a defence of behaviourism involves recourse to words like 'think it to be true', 'believe it' and so on – words which the strictures of behaviourism do not permit. How would a behaviourist describe Paul's conversion on the Damascus Road? That the organism was in motion, emitting negative responses to the conditioned stimuli called Christians but that the unconditioned stimulus of the bright light, taken together with the conditioned stimuli already present, produced a conditioned response which was positively reinforced by the voice from heaven and the subsequent ministrations of the organism called Ananias? What light is there in this? Who would be converted by it? On the more mundane level, there is, as Norman Malcolm once pointed out, something absurd about a psychological doctrine which suggests that I discover I am hungry when I find myself running home for lunch.

The fringe religions, cults, self-religions and semi-secular therapies are attempts to affirm individuality and feelings against the behaviourist's view of 'the empty organism'. They are a rebellion against the scientific dog-mas and assumptions in which our understanding of the world, and our self-understanding, are described. The trouble with the new religions and therapies is that they too give us a picture of mankind which is only a caricature. They are the spiritualized aspects of consumerism in which what matters most is *my* benefit, *my* salvation, 'getting my head together' as the hippie phrase used to say. And the range of benefits promised to the adherent is both narrow and shallow: instant enlightenment, instant community, instant renewal. The advertisements for these new reli-gions are exactly like the advertisements for anything else which appear on television. We are offered the best of both worlds in these advertisements where all is 'new' and 'exciting' but also 'safe' and 'familiar' – of the family, a key concept in all consumerism, advertising as it does safety, togetherness and the comfort of what is well-known while, at the same time, appealing to the largest possible audience: we all belong to some sort of family. So there are 'Family Services' in church, the 'Family Butcher' in the high street, 'Family Entertainment' on television, 'Family Barbecues' and 'Family Discos'. The word 'family' is priceless to the advertiser because it has a limitless connotation and therefore an infinite capacity to fix itself to any human emotion or desire. It connotes inclusivity because we are all members of a family, but also exclusivity because to be in a family means to be protected. It indicates mature and responsible relationships by suggesting husbands, wives, parents and so on, but also childishness – 'keep it in the family' and other sorts of indulgence. It connotes intense relationships since the procreation of children and the awesome rites of passage are truly familiar, but also shallowness – television calls this 'light' – and the cultivation of what is inoffensive, bland – as in 'Family Entertainment'. Many of the new religious groups thus offer a palatable delusion: excitement and safety, newness and familiarity.

The earlier Gnosticism offered redemption through committed membership to the group and to the secret doctrine. The new religions and therapies offer exactly the same. But committed earnestness among adherents should not be mistaken for Faustian or Augustinian singlemindedness or unity of purpose: for the essence of a sect is its self-understanding as belonging to what is restricted, exclusive, rarefied and above all secret. They will object and claim that their secret is an open secret. Anyone may join. But it is, in fact, still a formal logical secret precisely because only devotees have the private, sectarian language in which the secret is guarded and transmitted. The new religious groups notoriously put themselves beyond criticism and smile disdainfully, sometimes even pityingly, at ordinary mortals who have recourse only to common speech and who therefore cannot encroach on what is esoteric and occult. The language of critical appraisal is always general and so is the language of a national church, because a national church is the spiritual dimension of all the citizens, of all the language users. A true religion is a genuine civilization, a culture; the new groups turn away from the general culture which they claim to find wanting. They are, therefore, literally cults of their own imagining, occult.

The sectarians opposed by Irenaeus liked to call themselves 'Pneumatics' – those possessed of spirit. It was a way of putting themselves above criticism and therefore above authority; for as soon as their strange doctrines and typologies came under attack, they were able to appeal to their Spirit-guaranteed secret which ensured they were always in the right. It was a form of *hubris*. Contemporary sectarianism does exactly the same thing when it insists that only those who actually belong and are committed to the sect are in any position to know the truth. In extreme cases the Spirit is claimed exclusively and the sectarian language becomes truly private – as with the Charismatics who regard themselves as the true successors of first-century Christians and who speak in tongues incomprehensible to the outsider. This, it is true, is what parts of the early Church did. But there is no reasonable going back to those days: the Church is not now a sect but a spiritual dimension of a public reality, a nation, a civilization. Or it was until very recently. The return to sectarianism means the end of the Church and of the civilization, the culture. This is what St Paul knew even in the era of the early Church's sectarianism and that was why he cautioned those in Corinth who were so fond of speaking in tongues – for he knew that, if the Church was to succeed in the gentile nations, it must speak a public and not a private language. Paul claimed the gift of tongues for himself but his creative theological and missionary work was done in the public language of his day. His ambition for the gospel was that it should not create an enthusiastic sect but a universal Church. The gospel was no secret but something that could be demonstrated as true in practice to the experience of all men everywhere. That is the meaning of the Epistle to the Romans in which the religious experience of the Jews, up to and including the life of Christ, is claimed to be the experience of gentiles also. The gentiles were not given the Law written on tablets of stone but they knew, said Paul, in their consciences that the same Law was written on their hearts. 'All have sinned and fallen short of the glory of God.' 'As in Adam all men die, so in Christ shall all men be made alive.'

Today's pneumatics are encouraged by our bland technological utilitarianism and the mass-media operators, who have an interest in finding movements that are 'new' so that these can be talked about. The scripts for documentary programmes on sectarianism all sound alike whether the sect under observation is Bhagwan Rajneesh's Orange People or some novelty about diet. And the conclusion is always predictable: this sect or movement, these habits, may strike you as strange but, in our tolerant liberal society, we must allow people to make their own choices. The assumption is that none of the sects or fads does very much harm, and that they can certainly do no harm to *you* at all if you keep well clear of them. Whereas in fact, harm is being done constantly to public life by the socially realized superstition that truth can be apprehended in hundreds of uncritical and uncriticizable sects which, in the jargon of their private irrationalities, are in constant mutual contradiction. It is only the privacy of their languages which masks the contradictoriness. Once again the image is Babel. When the spiritual dimension of the culture was the English Church, debate about religious matters actually took place all the time. Not everyone was interested of course – why should they have been? But any who wished to inform themselves were able to do so. Social and political settlements and a shared identity were worked out in those debates. How can modern society expect to cohere when it is made up of mutually indifferent gangs of pneumatics, paternalistically surveyed by spiritless utilitarianism, by the always degenerating mass-media which observe all events from the point of view of 'light entertainment' and as opportunities for money-making?

Moreover, the notion of individual choice in the issue of which sect to join is illusory. Choice implies rational decision which in turn implies actual mental activity in the public language; but any right use of the public language immediately shows up the fatuousness of sectarianism. No one who understands the language given to him by our cultural tradition could be taken in for a moment by the neologizing sects. Could we imagine Dr Johnson as a Charismatic or Eliot as a follower of Guru Bhagwan? It is not a coincidence that our best creative writers have always been those who were aware of what was going on in the civilization as a whole. That awareness was what made their message truly universal. Sectarianism narrows the range of emotional response, calls for snap decisions between false polarities, and therefore at a stroke abolishes subtlety and nuance and our universal humanity. Subtlety and nuance, the power to discriminate, are necessary for good art to flourish. So we can understand why there is no Charismatic music of any value, no significant poetry or novels being written by the disciples of Bhagwan. Or how can a secular cult based upon an obsession with exercise or 'whole food' produce a language, let alone a literature, which is truly universal? They lack human fibre, these enthusiasts.

When the sectarians claim that their particular sect can only be appreciated by devotees, by people who have learned the language and joined the club, they are thereby guaranteeing that the initiate will turn his back on culture and civilization. For our culture is an attempt to contain and express all that is human, but the jargons of the sects simply cannot express the full range of our humanity. The initiate's linguistic, national and spiritual capacities become limited by the language of the sect and this in fact is what removes his capacity to choose. His capacity to reason about his initiation and the truth or falsity of the cult's ideas is concealed by his adopting the cultic language which performs a double negativity: it neither admits of any self-criticism nor ranges widely enough to take account of general or universal human experiences.

The new sectarianism then is antisocial and antihuman, a living denial of a unifying human experience. So it is bound to be anticultural, opposed to the best that has been thought and written about man's estate. This is what makes the cults aesthetically sordid and irrational; it also gives to them the idea that they exercise a superior moral authority over the rest of society. Tons of books, pamphlets, films, tapes and video cassettes are put out every year in the attempt to convert the rest of the naughty world to the higher insights generated by Guru Whatsisname or by the Church of St Knees Up and All Change. This stuff is of appalling quality. How could it be otherwise when those who write it have rejected the common experiences which alone make quality a living possibility? But the intellectual impoverishment is the form in which is cast their moral imperatives without which, allegedly, the rest of us are on the primrose path to the everlasting bonfire – though they would not put it in just those terms. But if they cannot talk sense, why should we believe in their assumed moral authority? Moral truths, like any other truths, are not expressed by poor arguments, slipshod prose, failed music and ignoble words. Any group which is intellectually vacuous and aesthetically vulgar is bound to be morally torpid.

According to the sectarians' moral doctrines, the rest of humanity is under judgement: it may be the notion of a last judgement at the end of time or of some perpetual existential crisis like being unfulfilled. The logical error upon which this sectarian morality is based is contained in their assumption that knowledge about any sort of judgement can be acquired without recourse to the public language of criticism. But even the word 'judgement' comes from the same word as 'criticism'. If the sectarians have no principles of criticism when it comes to dealing with the ordinary things of this world, why should we believe them when they pretend to speak to us of a judgement which is spiritual and eternal? A prominent sectarian once wrote to tell me that I would be sent to hell because of my criticisms of his movement. Well, I believe that my criticisms were valid because, in so far as I can tell, they were based on the idea that the only way to proceed is in the logic of the common language. Whereas, I could show in the common language and beyond doubt that my adversary's arguments were incoherent. His only escape from the argument was to lapse into his uncommon, sectarian jargon and all its private assumptions. Now, if my arguments were valid, do I still go to hell? By this point, I want to argue that moral authority is not possible without intellectual clarity. We may not command what is incoherent.

That which is intellectually vapid and morally incoherent is bound to be spiritually empty. How can I be 'fulfilled' by what is empty? The sectarian claims about the perpetual judgement under which we labour are as bogus as their claims about the last judgement. We are not made whole by the assumption of aesthetic awareness and moral sense. Abundant life means life that is full. To claim the Spirit while denying the mind and the body is only to talk hot air. But the followers of Divine Light make the aim of their spirituality 'getting rid of mind'. Another revivalist wrote to tell me that my strictures on his movement were 'only arguments'. What was his letter stating this opinion if not an argument to persuade me I was in the wrong? But his ostensible use of the common language was rootless. Behind his words lay the authority of the esoteric, occult experience. That experience is spurious, because it is not part of our common language, common life.

Irenaeus spent his life tilting against the Gnostics and in particular against those who claimed that the end of the world was at hand. Apocalyptic groups must always be resisted because by looking to an experience of imminent final catastrophe they distract our attention from the proper business of this life. And, once again, the so called 'knowledge' that the world is coming to an end is only spurious. How could anyone know this except by an appeal to esoteric, private wisdom? There is no such privileged insight. Wisdom is the product of sustained concentration on the whole experience of what it is to be a human being; as we have seen, the manufactured language of the sects is too restricted to contain that experience. Two questions arise out of the idea of the apocalypse.

First, does it matter? It may seem odd to claim that the end of the world is an insignificant event, but we can only judge its significance if we can know what the expression 'the end of the world' means. This is no mere exercise in Logical Positivism but an acknowledgement that even the most lurid concepts expressed in the floweriest language should not beguile us if, when we look closely at them, we see that they are incoherent. Nonsense remains nonsense even when it is couched in the style of sub-poetic effusiveness. 'The end of the world you say, Sir? Why, that's a fine sounding phrase to stop the conversation at dinner! I will lay down my knife and fork this instant while you explain it to me.'

If 'the end of the world' means we are all going to die, it

is no more than we knew already. The fact that we are all to die in the same moment makes no difference; indeed some have even drawn a certain comfort and solidarity from the prospect. 'We'll all go together when we go.' The end of the world is not something that can happen to us as individuals. As with the individual life, so with the life of the world, Wittgenstein's saying remains true: 'Death is not an event *in* life'. I do not experience the end. I die. And I shall die in any case, end or no end.

But the apocalyptic evangelists claim to know what happens after the end, and they urge me to prepare properly for the end, because how I prepare will affect what happens to me after the end. 'After the end', an odd phrase, one which is necessarily tied to a literalistic interpretation of prophetic utterance. We saw in Chapter 3 that the literalistic interpretation is a false one, because incoherent. 'He ascended into heaven' cannot be made to mean so literally in English unless heaven is in the sky. So, if it means anything, it must mean something else. The same holds true for all the prophecies of the end. I do not believe that we shall actually and corporeally 'be caught up to meet the Lord in the air'. A literal belief in that phrase entails the idea that the Lord is up in the sky; and he assuredly is not. Similarly, the 'heavenly city' and the 'lake of fire' are not places in the ordinary sense of that word.

Still, the apocalypse is a doctrine which says something true. It says we live under judgement, always and between the fire of love and the fires of hell. This judgement is defined by our true end – an 'end' not in terms of a phantasmagoria appropriate to treatment by Hollywood, but 'end' in the sense of *telos*, final purpose. And to say this is not to make the doctrine of less effect, to water it down; for how could a notion of reward and punishment 'after death' – whatever that might mean – be of greater ethical significance than the constant demand that we discover our true end in this daily life? If apocalyptic theories were true in the literal sense, they would only serve to devalue the importance of this life. How can I be totally committed to what is only a preparation for the real thing? It is morally necessary for us to know that we are not just in the Prologue but in the Play.

The second and more important question about apocalyptic groups concerns the way in which their persuasion generates in them a contemptuous attitude towards people in general. As George Eliot says in *Middlemarch*: 'They are a narrow ignorant set, and do more to make their neighbours uncomfortable than to make them better. Their system is a sort of wordly-spiritual cliqueism: they really look on the rest of mankind as a doomed carcase which is to nourish them for heaven.' Again this is the unmistakable spirit of sectarianism, and the will to power seeking to exert authority over others by the pretension to privileged insights and by scaremongering. By their gnosis they claim to be able to escape the awful fate which is about to descend on mankind; and we too can be saved only by the willing forfeit of our common humanity and its public language and by acceptance of the restricted code of the sect. The sect never doubts its own wisdom, never imagines that truth may be of more general application than to the support of private opinions.

In our own day apocalyptic groups have undergone a transmutation by means of technology and secularization. The concept of the end of the world has incarnated itself in the substance of the bomb and chemical warfare. Apocalyptic groups which once huddled together to await the last moment on mountain tops, now march through the streets with banners of protest. Lament about the end has become righteous indignation at its prospect. In a materialistic, utilitarian age the end is not seen as inevitable but as something which may be prevented. In the century of practical atheism, the end and the Last Judgement have slipped from the hand of God into the hands of men. In

Answer to Job, Jung writes, 'For the dark God has slipped the atom bomb and chemical weapons into his hands and given him the power to empty out the apocalyptic vial of wrath on his fellow creatures'. Because the means to the end are now in our own hands, it is thought by some that we can prevent its occurrence. Principal among contemporary apocalyptic groups is the Campaign for Nuclear Disarmament.

CND differs from ancient apocalyptic groups in that it does not seek to gloat over the likely fate of the damned: after all, we shall all be damned in a moment's fire which burns more brightly than the unquenchable lake, or the cold of a nuclear winter more icy and desolate than anything in Dante. No, it is not CND's good will which is in doubt, but their inability or unwillingness to see the dark aspect of man's volition. This is what puts the movement on a footing with earlier apocalyptic sects – the partial vision, the restricted language and the inadequate psychology which must follow from these things. By concentrating their attention on the end as an event in time, members of CND omit to study man's end as *telos* (the true end or purpose). Any study of man's *telos* must involve a study of man's nature. A study of man's nature reveals the Pauline dilemma: 'The thing I would not, that I do; and what I would, I do not.' The issue is not of whether, as a matter of tactics, we *should* ban the bomb, but whether we *can* ban the bomb. The early Gnostic and apocalyptic groups opposed by Irenaeus believed that they had the key to knowledge which would deliver them from wrath and punishment. They also disregarded the effects of sin. It is hard to avoid the comparison with our CND who, though in much altered circumstances, seem to be making the same sort of claim exactly: this gnosis, banning the bomb, is true gnosis; moreover we are able to put it into practice. Whereas, the study of man in his individual sinfulness, original and unoriginal, striving yet erring, and of man with his corporate warlike history, reveals a creature limited by the bounds of his own imperfection. The doctrine that evil is either illusory or of no effect is a Gnostic, Marcionite, doctrine which has often been condemned by orthodoxy. Because man's basic experience does not much change, the shape of his mind does not change and the same solutions and half solutions to his psychological and spiritual problems re-emerge over millennia. And so we find the Gnostic heresy alive and well and living outside wire fences at air bases throughout the country.

These sorts of remarks are not welcomed by CND. They repudiate them with the claim that they are at least 'doing something'. But what if the 'something' is the wrong thing – and I leave aside entirely the question of whether the *tactics* of unilateral disarmament would prevent rather than cause war – what would be the point in doing the wrong thing, how ever well-intentioned the doer? Proceeding on the basis of a false or inadequate view of man's end and nature can only lead to more confusion; and confusion is the climate in which wars best flourish.

I do not wish to end this chapter with a counsel of despair, though perhaps some measure of despair is called for when we have regard to man's condition. Besides, I believe that nuclear war is not the worst thing that can happen to a man and to his society. The worst that can happen is that he and his contemporaries lose contact with the meaning and tradition of their civilization and culture, that they cease to ask the purifying and renewing question, 'What mean these stones?' And it is also true that the events of Babel were part of the unruliness which provoked the Flood. Are we afraid to die in a nuclear war? Are we not dead already if our lives are lived out in banality, in obeisance to the trivia of television and consumerism? Like the soap opera characters in that American film about nuclear war, *The Day After*, we have nothing to lose in the conflagration for we have surrendered all willingly already. CND speaks of 'the tragedy of nuclear war' but the tragedy occurred when we lost contact with the roots that clutch; evidence of this loss is all around us in our schools, homes, public houses, churches, at our seaside resorts, in the shops we visit, the books and newspapers we read. It is fashionable – another instance of the Marcionite heresy – to deny the power of the devil. C. H. Sisson warns us of Satan's continuing potency and even tells us where he is to be found in contemporary actuality: there in the corner of every suburban lounge within the cabinet and behind the screen lurks 'The Prince of this World' before whom all pay homage.

The task before us is not the prevention of the end but the rediscovery of our *telos*. In the next and final chapter I should like to suggest a way in which we might make a beginning.

'In my beginning is my end.'

6
The Language of God

The problem is of how to live any sort of spiritual life in a world made crass by mechanism, of how to relearn the language of God in the new Babel. To return to Carlyle's phrase, what can it possibly mean to love God 'in an atheistic century'? Augustine said our hearts are restless until they rest in God. How do we find God and trust him unreservedly in an age which has subverted all our speech about him? Even the question sounds coy. If the true end of man is to 'praise and glorify God for ever', how can we begin to go about this in the century after the death of God, in a fragmented culture where even the ancient truths are at best regarded as matters of private opinion about which anyone may 'make up his own mind'? How to find the peace that passeth all understanding in a world of general indifference and noise?

I have tried to show that we do not, in fact, 'make up our own minds'. Our minds are made up of what goes into them, and we are what we imbibe. What we imbibe, therefore, decides what manner of people we become. Minds must be filled with something whether it be liturgical poetry or the contents of the colour supplements. Where do we begin? Eliot says we begin with the dead – a phrase which will provoke instant scorn in the modern Church and the modern world which feel so certain of their grip on life, liveliness, all things 'new', 'positive', 'relevant' and 'meaningful'. What Eliot means, of course – if I may use another tainted word – is that we begin with our tradition. To say this is almost as bad as to say that we 'die with the dying', or that 'we are born with the dead'. For a world which dare not face death can never experience the resurrection of the dead. And that is the nature of our difficulties about the resurrection: these masquerade as intellectual problems, analysis, conjuring tricks with logic; but their real origin is our failure to feel the truth of life out of death within ourselves. We lack the experience and so we miss the meaning.

We begin with our tradition. This is a hard saying in a climate which seeks to foster the very opposite: all things 'new', 'up front' and definitely untraditional. Even the salesmen for what is bang up to date – the writers of those colour supplements, the advertising men, the liturgical revisers and so on – cannot quite escape the influence of tradition. They nod half-respectfully towards it before spending their time translating it, putting it 'in a language which people of today can understand'. It is to say, 'Let us have all the benefits of tradition without having to put up with tradition itself'. This is not possible – because form and content are inseparable, and if we change the form we thereby change the content. The first mistake is to assume that there is a language which 'people of today' understand and into which tradition can be translated without loss. The clearest demonstration of this mistake is done by considering the case of music: no one thinks that Mozart's B flat piano concerto or Beethoven's Ninth Symphony can be modernized, simplified so that they become 'meaningful' for today's listeners. In fact, any attempt to make Mozart's works more simple is bound only to make them more complicated, since his art consists in inspired lucidity. And we do not start with an 'understanding' of Mozart's music before ever having heard a note of it. We listen to it again and again until its nature becomes clear to us. We learn by repetition. And the repetition must be of the same thing, the thing itself. We cannot learn Mozart by hearing not-Mozart.

As David Martin has said, 'The question of absolute intelligibility and clarity is not the first question. The mind begins in incantation and then approaches comprehension.' Only fashionable educational theories, which have even extended as far as the compilers of modern liturgies, want us to understand *before* we have experienced. But there is no understanding without standing-under. This is very demanding of course, but so many of those who stand over us – teachers, parsons, liturgical revisers, programme makers, television personalities – demand that everything be undemanding. The unfamiliar has no place in Family Entertainment. But the stuff that is undemanding is quite literally that: it demands nothing of *us*. So we give nothing. So we receive nothing in return. We forget that everything was unfamiliar once. Congregations complain, 'We didn't know that hymn you chose, Vicar!' But there was a time when they did not even know 'The Lord is My Shepherd'. Our whole language had to be learned from *nothing*. And we know it *by heart*.

There is a popular argument which asks why we should bother ever to learn anything that is difficult, demanding. Why not be content instead with what is easy, effortless and undemanding? The answer again is that we are created out of what we imbibe. What would it be like to be only a ragbag of the latest pop-songs and catchphrases, to have our rational faculties defined by the editorial columns of the gutter press and our emotional lives shaped by paperback confessions of the cinema's fading lovelies and characters from soap opera? Well, we know what it is like because we see the evidence all around. 'I had not known death had undone so many.'

This is not élitism, mere culture-vulturism as if from an assumed position of refined sensibility one were permitted to hold the general populace in mute contempt. There are those who should be held in contempt and these are the people in authority and power, blind guides, bad shepherds and hirelings, who continually foist on the people what will not sustain them. It is deprivation by excess. Whereas it is the duty of those who have been educated, that is drawn out, extended and fulfilled by what they have learned, to help others become similarly fulfilled. If I cite the second of Christ's commandments first, this is what is meant by loving our neighbour as ourselves. 'Feed my sheep.' The Church, to its credit, has shown signs of doing this in sacks of wheat. When is it going to relearn the meaning of providing sustenance in things of the mind and spirit? But this is not the Church's task only, though it is the Church's task *par excellence*; it is a universal, because human, responsibility.

A friend argued with me: 'You're not there to make them cultured but to make them holy'. It is a false distinction. The two are the same thing. I offered a working description of holiness as 'experience charged with reality to the greatest possible extent'. The question is of locating that reality. Its location is readily found in the master-works of our culture and tradition. And the reality we find there is a fully human reality, an artistic and creative incarnation of the most complete understanding of what it is to be a man in time. Beside *Hamlet* and *Don Giovanni*, the soap operas are idolatrous because they profane the nature of man who is made in the image of God. What is it really like to be a man? Well, we know something about this from our daily experience of real life, but how can we measure and judge the value of our experience – the one thing necessary, living a good life – unless we have some standard which will act as a guide? The only way to do this is to become acquainted with the best that our culture has achieved and to enter its world. There is nowhere else to go except the outer darkness.

But how do we know which things are 'the best'? To begin with we do not know. We 'do Shakespeare' at school. We sit bored and uncomprehending through *Hamlet* and, if all the usual influences go unmitigated, we decide that Shakespeare is not for us. But if we persevere, see the

99

play over and over again, read the text, speak aloud some of the words, learn them by rote so we know them by heart, we come to find that the shape, rhythm and sense of the play – *its world* – is alive in us. A new depth is reached, a new dimension added. This is very demanding, of course. But what is demanded is more than repaid because the masterpiece gives us new resources on which we can depend, and which enlarge and extend (educate) our understanding of ourselves and the world. Because art is not theory or explanations or abstract principles, but image and icon, the incarnation of spirit into character and substance, this understanding is not merely theoretical like Casaubon's 'key to all mythologies'. Great art increases the personality, enriches the soul, makes us more than we were. It makes us whole, holy.

The masterpieces of our cultural tradition have the power to make us whole. They are in nature sacramental. They do this by enclosing height and depth in a single piece. Every masterpiece represents a transcendence of opposition, because the creative genius explores beyond the limits of his former perception and so extends the boundaries of what can be said, what can be felt. So, when we read the play or hear the music, our own personal horizons are extended. We learn to incorporate what is strange, other, holy and so we become charged with reality to a greater extent. And the supreme delight of this experience comes through the realization that what we have incorporated, what lives in us, yet remains strange and holy. No wonder we speak of artistic enchantment. No wonder Kierkegaard said of Mozart, 'Thou who has ensured I have not passed through this world without having been moved by something.' That is it, exactly: being moved, *transported*, from where we were to a new location. And this is always demanding. Often it is labour without light. As Eliot says, 'To get from where you are to where you are not, you must go by a way in which there is no ecstasy.' Ecstasy is arrival.

The genius's work is a truly unifying symbol because he himself first experiences and then expresses the polarities. And the truth of this unity is always incarnation. Nothing is gained by saying, 'This is what the play is *about*.' We can only attend to the whole, concentrate, appropriate the whole action. We are not looking for morals but for life. Sisson wrote, 'A moral saw is not worth an I see.' The 'message' we derive from the masterpieces is not a piece of moral advice – as if one might remark after seeing *Julius Caesar*, 'Ah, so that's what becomes of you if you get too ambitious!' The whole message and meaning of great art is simply that these heights have been scaled, these depths plumbed, these experiences exist. And, in the unifying power of genius, they are transcended: 'The fire and the rose are one'.

Truth as mere explanation of the world in propositions, formulae, has no place in the great work of art – which presents the world itself. The great epic dramas are not 'stories with a meaning', still less are they tales with a moral. As Hazlitt wrote of Shakespeare: 'The ethical delineations of that noble and liberal casuist do not exhibit the drab-coloured quakerism of morality. His plays are not copies from *The Whole Duty of Man*, or from *The Academy of Compliments*'. The spiritual power of such as those great plays is revealed in their inexhaustibility. We can never rest secure in a single judgement of them, as if to say, 'So Hamlet should have believed the ghost. He should not have hesitated!' Or 'Lear ought to have trusted Cordelia from the beginning!' The plays exceed our judgement because the language of inspired imagination exceeds the language of criticism. Or we look at Raphael's Madonna and Child. What meets us in that picture is not an opinion but another sort of glory – indubitability. We look and we know that we are facing a human truth which is more than propositional truth. It is truth as the incarnation of spiritual reality. We do not judge great art. It judges us.

The best writing, the greatest pictures and the finest music cannot be gainsaid, bypassed or encompassed by less noble creations. This is why art is always superior to criticism – though criticism, by appropriating the objects of its study, can approach art, can become something like an art. But the vocabulary of all criticism and appreciation of art is provided by art itself. The best writing is, after all, simply the best that can be said; the best pictures are the clearest vision of what is true; the best music defines and sets in order our relation to all other sounds. I feel I am only stating the obvious: the best is the best – what other standard could there be? Great art is inspired, which is to say it is the language of God.

There is here an enormous difficulty, for great art is also the language of the Devil, and necessarily so because Satan too is part of creation. Evil is a fact in the world. Any art which does not portray evil as well as good is bound to fail. Indeed, good can only be seen to shine in its full glory when it is contrasted with the darkness of evil. How could we have known the depth of MacDuff's courage if we had not first become aware of Macbeth's depravity? And yet that play is never pornographic: it gives full weight to reality, to the world of men and princes as that world is. Pornography and puritanism are species of the same thing: shallowness, caricature. By leaving out 'what some might find offensive' or by elaborating on artificial sensuality, they distort reality: that is, they lie. For aspects of reality do in fact offend us: sickness, pain, betrayal, bereavement, death. If art is to make us whole it must include and transform evil. The way in which art does transform evil is not by providing an endless series of happy endings but by actually depicting evil in all its horribleness. To portray evil is to comprehend it, to encompass it; and that comprehension must be, therefore, something which happens on a deeper level than evil acts themselves. To comprehend perfectly, to portray compellingly, to depict indubitably – these are the ways of transcendence.

It is sometimes objected that this is to claim too much for art, to make morality and religion only aspects of aesthetics. Why do we need art to sharpen our moral awareness and to enliven our spiritual senses when we can gain experience of good and evil, the polarities, at first hand in daily life? We can, of course, gain this experience but our apprehension is always duller than that of the man of genius and his portrayal of reality is to be allowed to guide our own. If this were not true, then art would be only an interesting diversion, a pretty puzzle to beguile the time. When we come into contact with the works of Mozart and Shakespeare, we know directly that such a view of the status of art is absurd.

When art shows us the polarities, good and evil, it rarely shows them as entirely distinct and separate entities. Despite the puritan's craving for sweetness and light and for the long procession of happy endings, and despite the pornographer's interest in only what is sordid, real life brutally refuses to be depicted in that way. Real art shows us good and evil bound up together. Our greatest artistic creation is tragedy, and tragedy's substance is the inescapable consequence of evil effects even to a man who is good. For no ordinary man represents goodness unmixed, not even Job himself. And tragic art is a dramatic working of Paul's great psychological truth: 'The good I would, that I do not; the evil I would not, that I do'. It is the human condition to be, as someone remarked of *Oliver Twist*, 'half golden, half rotten'. Our earliest fiction says as much: man, made in the image of God is yet fallen into the deepest sin. Again the two heroes appear – the Irenaean and the Augustinian man.

The masterpieces of our culture are not there as attempts

to paper over the great crack which is Original Sin. To imagine that is what they are for is mere aestheticism, art as diversion and wishful thinking, a delightful frisson to distract us from vile bodies and the inescapable tomb. Great art always sustains and intensifies the pull of the polarities, showing us that salvation in this world is never unmingled joy. The relentless faithfulness of art to human experience will not allow us the caricature redemption of the smiling saved. Salvation includes suffering, and in this life it always will. There is no passage, by artistic encouragement or by any other means, to gardens of perfect peace to 'long hoped for calm, the autumnal serenity and the wisdom of age'. But another kind of salvation is possible for everyone; it belongs with the acceptance of the reality of human experience, bad and good; and the acceptance is the salvation. Not quietism, but 'Thy will not mine be done'. This is the attitude, the prayer, which actually alters reality and delivers us from the bondage of anxiety. But never completely, for we are not able, as fallen creatures, to sustain the pure intention of that prayer for very long. The anxiety returns, worse. We cry out, 'My God, why hast thou forsaken me?' See what good company we keep! That prayer or attitude is able to alter reality for us because it calls for a revolutionary shift in our centre of consciousness, from I to Not-I or rather from I to Thou. As Kierkegaard said, 'Most men are objective towards others and subjective towards themselves. The real task is to become objective towards oneself and subjective towards others.' 'Thy will not mine be done' is the will to see ourselves from a point outside our egotistical absorption – a Christian might say 'from God's point of view'; but the reality of the psychological shift is undeniable whatever anyone's religious pretensions may be.

This is not a method of ego-extinction, since it is the ego, I, which speaks the words of that great prayer. It is rather the willing acceptance by the ego of a perspective wider than its own. And the will is weak – so weak that it deserted even Christ in that cry of dereliction from the cross. Our will is weak. We try and fail, strive and err, but we are not totally depraved and the image of God within us is not obliterated by Original Sin.

I have mentioned that prayer of Christ in the garden as a prelude to trying to summarize my belief that his story, of all stories, is the cultural creation *par excellence*. It is the story which resides in the very depths of our civilization's experience. It has defined our culture and in words, music and pictures, it forms the shape and substance of our minds. I am saying, then, that Christian faith in some form is inescapable for anyone brought up in our culture. Or I should say *was* inescapable until very recently, for there are now forces loose in our society which threaten to unhinge every kind of rational connection, every possibility of sustained and ordered thought about anything which cannot be pressed into a two minutes news summary among the pop records, a 'slot' or an 'item' on the children's television programme, or which cannot be answered in a sentence by the guest on the chat show.

This means that the first task for spirituality in the new Babel – for even the possibility of *any* sort of spirituality – must be one of relentless criticism. The whole force of our minds and all the resources of our language must be turned upon the exposure and rejection of what is shallow, anti-human and barbarous. For if the forms which can contain and shape spiritual life are allowed to be replaced by the 'format' of sheer banality that is all-pervasive, then our culture can be described only as having reached a last dead end. Where there is no rational form, but only a mindless babble of words and other noises and a confusion of rapid images, there is no possibility of a mental and spiritual life of any sort. Let barbarism in pubs and churches, schools and supermarkets be objected to. Let the television companies and the so-called 'local' radio stations (which nevertheless all continue to sound exactly the same) be told that the world is too interesting and important to be treated as they treat it. These are all acts of cultural – and therefore moral and religious – conservation. They are today's equivalent of throwing the moneychangers out of the temple. Moreover, all this has to be done in circumstances which are far from propitious. The forces of chaos – the waters and the flood which followed the first Babel – are overwhelming. But some resistance can be mounted, some criticism made. 'For us there is only the trying. The rest is not our business.' Not to do anything is cultural and spiritual suicide for, since the conditions for a sustaining spiritual life barely exist, we must recreate them or become spiritually dead.

But there is another level, deeper than that of protest and criticism. It is nothing less than the appropriation by each individual of the creative centrality of English Christianity, not an impossible task, quite; for copies of the King James Bible and the Book of Common Prayer are still to be had and churches which have not adopted the 'format' of 'Family Entertainment' may still be found, here and there. It is asking a lot to expect folk who have lived most of their lives in this secularized bedlam to open the Prayer Book and to read the Psalms set for each day, to follow the Collects, Epistles and Gospels throughout the year. And then there is the delicate issue of agnosticism: it is thought to be insulting to ask today's refined sensitivity to focus on something to do with religion; for religion is almost universally regarded as one of the childish things which we have put away. But if we will not give our attention to English Christianity – a tradition which has shaped minds and created our speech for hundreds of years – it is interesting to notice what does receive our attention. What irony when progressive parents do not much approve of their children being taught the story of Jesus as if it were true, but rather applaud when they are served up the mish-mash of comparative religions and philosophies! 'Some people believe this, Sharon, and others that, while of course there are those who believe nothing: tell me, what do *you* believe?' How can she tell unless she has first been introduced to a world, to a consistent language, a culture, a cosmos not a chaos? If school assembly and public prayer can be described, as I have heard it described often, as a symptom of bias and prejudice, a kind of indoctrination, what words are there left to describe what is allowed to take place without objection – not just the infants' and juniors' supermarket of religion but the obsession with technology and computers, the willingness to let children fall under the unbridled influence of television as junk which I described in chapter two? It may be that the Christian faith and all its works can be rejected, but the rejection, if it is to be persuasive, must be on the basis of something more coherent than fashionable agnosticism and uninformed indifference. Yes, there must be indoctrination – the putting in of some doctrine – because, whether the fact pleases us or not, something or other *will* go into children's heads. Why should we squander the choice of what this is to be?

Much of the contemporary world's objection to traditional Christianity is based on the idea that the faith must be understood, analysed and accepted before it is practised. This seems to me to be a mistake. It is not a question of deciding anything beforehand from an 'objective' position; as in the case of appreciating the great art of our civilization, it is a matter of entering a world, appropriating certain experiences and learning by heart. This is how any language is learned and it is how we learn the language of the spirit, the language of God. We enter the Church's year, that sequence of festivals and fasts, and we submit to its rhythms. These days the word 'submit' is not well liked, but, as minds must be filled with *something*, personalities will also surely be governed and directed by some rhythm, some pattern of events. Is it too outrageous to suggest that the rhythm and pattern we may find most helpful is that of the Christian faith in the English cultural tradition? I am not urging enthusiasm and missionary zeal, but a quiet and restrained acquaintance with the words, actions and observances which belong in the creative depth of our language and whole way of life. Where else is there to go?

All the most important psychological insights of our civilization can be found in the Book of Common Prayer. It defines the spirituality of the Englishman. Modern psychology knows that depressive illness can be at least partly relieved by being articulated. This doctrine is enshrined in the Prayer Book in words of extraordinary weight and power. Are we depressed, out of sorts, alienated as any of Beckett's tramps? No words express this predicament better than, 'Man that is born of a woman hath but a short time to live and is full of misery. He cometh up, and is cut down, like a flower; he fleeth as it were a shadow and never continueth in one stay. In the midst of life we are in death.' Could anything be more poignant, or simpler? Those words need no translation into a language 'relevant to the needs of today'. They are mostly words of one syllable. And their rhythm is alive, exciting, as if we are following the footsteps of one walking through the valley of the shadow. Are they even better than valium, stress-counselling and electric shock? There is nothing in those words to strain our scrupulous agnosticism. Nothing there which we cannot *believe*. How can we doubt what is indubitable?

Systematic attempts to doubt what is indubitable are made nonetheless and these appear frequently in the therapies of modern psychology. Freudian theory knew about the need to look into our dark origins, into the unconscious blackness of the Id, if we are to achieve wholeness of being. Much of Freudian psychology is, in fact, remarkably

similar to the Christian understanding of man: the persist-
ence and power of libidinous energy and its dark side; the
need for catharsis which involves something like acknowl-
edging and bewailing sin; even the necessity to understand
those deep changes which occur in infancy – you must
become as a little child. Freud's later theory, which ex-
pounded a new idea about the structure of the personality,
contains echoes, in the language of Ego, Superego and Id,
of Augustine's psychological adaptation of the doctrine of
the Trinity, of *amor dei* and *amor sui*. But more recent
theories of personality – where these even acknowledge
that there is something which can be called 'personality' –
leave out the dark side of human nature. Drug therapies
and exercises in operant conditioning, electric shocks and
the like do not regard psychological disturbance as a
symptom of a moral problem. So how can these methods
hope to understand a human being at depth? For the glory
and curse of man is his capacity for moral choices, his will.
'See I set before you this day life and death, good and evil:
therefore choose good that you may live.' The tree in the
garden. But that is dismissed as *only* a myth!

Unlike the Prayer Book, the modern schools of psychology degrade psychology by making it into something
which is less than human. Patients must not be insulted by
anything so sordid and old-fashioned as a sense of sin. So
the new theories are 'non-judgemental'. Yes, and that
interesting word can be interpreted to mean 'not judging
the mind'. What is a psychology which does not judge the
mind? Mindless. Well, that is not to cast a slur; it is what
Behaviourism boasts. To abolish mind is to shut out the
moral faculty, to put oneself beyond good and evil. They
are proud of the fact that they no longer include the moral
dimension in their therapies because to associate sickness
and sin, physical disease with moral unease, is now regarded as no more than to entertain a primitive superstition. But if man's wickedness may not be discussed, what is

man's goodness worth? Nothing. And it cannot be spoken of by theorists who dare not name its necessary contrast – evil. Are we all only good now? But how can we tell, by what scale of value? If all the money is counterfeit, 'counterfeit' means nothing.

Everywhere in our society, the psychology of the Prayer Book is rejected – with what chaotic results as are apparent. The Prayer Book's view of man is honest and true. It sees him as divided in himself between will and desire, as often frustrated by his own failings about which, however, he is able to do very little. But it is not a mean, pessimistic book, for it sees man also as a member of Christ, a child of God and an inheritor of the Kingdom of heaven; the one who is made to be crowned with glory and honour above the angels. Its literalistic detractors want to know whether there are such things as angels, whether there is a heaven, a Christ or a God. They fail to see that the precise choice of words here is of less importance than the experienced spiritual realities to which these words refer. Why cannot these so-called 'scientific' detractors be thoroughgoing in the application of their own method? That is to say, why cannot they read what it says about the experience of being human in the Prayer Book and then discover in their own daily lives whether it is or is not telling the truth? Use the book as a working hypothesis. And find there both Augustine and Faust.

The loss of a true vision of our psychology, our spirituality, leads to the loss of personality's integrity. To believe what is not true about human personality is bound to lead to neurosis, personal dis-integration. Personal disintegration on the grand scale means a sick society. This is what we have got: abuse of sex and fear of death. Society treats sex as a plaything and no longer as a great mystery of communion. Death it cannot avoid, no, not even aided by behaviourism, which denies the personality even in this life, and abetted by a new liturgy which says that in suitable cases the words 'ashes to ashes, dust to dust' may be omitted. So society excludes death, removes all its associations from public view. No corpses in front parlours these days. And the ritual at the crematorium is designed to conceal as much as possible of death's reality: the extraordinary cleanliness, the disappearance of the coffin at the press of a button, untouched by human hand. The coffin is not laid to any final rest in public view. It simply goes behind a curtain instead. The ultimate is made only penultimate.

The disintegrated society hides its true nature from itself by a barrage of euphemisms. No 'corpses' or 'vile bodies' but, as Waugh noticed, only 'loved ones' and 'the deceased' who has not died but merely 'passed away'. The King James Bible speaks of Lazarus, 'He stinketh'. The Revised Standard Version says only, 'There will be an odour'. In the municipal crematorium there will not even be that. And we dare not face a Prayer Book which has the courage and honesty to say 'Worms destroy this body'. But modern society prides itself most of all on its honesty and openness, looking down on all past societies as eras of hypocrisy when the muck was swept under the carpet. So far have we passed into self-deception that we no longer even believe there is any muck.

The euphemism is a retreat from reality. To refuse to call things by their proper names is to distance oneself from the basic particulars which shape our natural and moral lives. The euphemism, as a refusal to face facts, indicates a neurotic civilization and culture. When 'promiscuity' and 'fornication' are words which have disappeared from common speech, there is no doubt that we are trying to conceal from ourselves the truth about our sexual proclivities. For the modern world has removed sex from the realm of ethics. 'Adultery' has lost the numinous ring which always surrounded it in the now unread and unspoken Ten Commandments, and the word is now no more than a technicality useful when it comes to procuring a divorce. The removal of sex from the moral sphere is a far more serious and far-reaching development than the psychologists' and psychotherapists' amoralizing of distress. Sexual acts are inevitably fastened to all that is most basic about human conduct and personality. We are talking first of all of a highly charged emotional experience: what does it mean to remove emotions from the sphere of morality? Is it not bound to lead to personal and social disaster? 'Do what you like about your feelings. There's nothing wrong with that. No one is going to be "judgemental".'

Secondly, what does it mean to remove from the moral sphere an act which not infrequently leads to the procreation of children? In the age of easy contraception, the begetting of children has become separated from its historic connection with the *purpose* of sex. So many babies are now regarded as problems, the unfortunate consequences of a malfunction of the Malthusian Belt, as Huxley might have said. It is no use saying that sex need not be associated with the purpose of procreation and that, in any case, the Pill makes such an association practically unnecessary; the natural order of things guarantees that the connection is always there. To move away from what is natural is to turn aside from what is real and the avoidance of the connection between facts and morals, by the pernicious doctrine of the Naturalistic Fallacy, is to base human conduct on unreality and abstract principle. It is ironic that information about sexual relationships used to be referred to as telling children 'the facts of life'.

Thirdly, it is easy to show that adultery cannot possibly shed its moral connection. It is always wrong and our language is what reveals this fact. It is wrong because it involves desertion, permanent or temporary, lies, deceit, betrayal and promise-breaking. How could promise-breaking ever be justified as a moral principle, as a guide to action? The 'permissive society' gets round this, as we have seen, by removing the concept of adultery and therefore, by implication, the idea of promise-breaking from the vocabulary of morals. This is impossible in practice. There can be no society in which promise-breaking is not *constitutive* of morality. When there is no taboo on the breaking of promises and vows, then the language itself breaks down. 'There is no moral compulsion to keep your promises'. 'But what else should I do with them? A "promise" means something that must be kept'. To say that promises need not be kept is therefore, first of all, a logical mistake arising out of the misuse of language. The consistent and widespread misuse of language can lead only to social and moral chaos – Babel.

The Prayer Book service for the Solemnization of Matrimony has such a firm hold on the nature of human psychology that its introduction spells out the purpose and meaning of that union. Marriage is 'a remedy against sin, and to avoid fornication'. No euphemisms there. No attempt to evade the truth about human nature. Men do have 'carnal lusts'. Do the compilers of the new liturgies which omit reference to these facts imagine that in these delicate and sensitive times our lives are lived out in ethereality? Or, by refusing to make mention of lust, do they mean to suggest it is something we can ignore? Can they themselves ignore it? That would make them into very extraordinary people – certainly too extraordinary to be allowed to draw up a form of *common* prayer.

I do not mean to suggest that in Cranmer's time everyone behaved themselves impeccably. Of course they did not, and the two Confessions in the Prayer Book indicate well enough that sin was always rife. But at least the old book was not afraid of the fact. The difference between right and wrong was set down and it is clear from the words in the rest of the book that there were entertained no sanctimonious illusions that people would always do what is right. The provision of those words 'acknowledge and bewail' in connection with sins whose burden could be felt as 'intolerable' and 'the remembrance of them grievous' does not indicate men of such incorporeal sensitivity as to imagine wickedness altogether purged from the world. By making so light with sin, do the modern liturgists want to suggest that sin is not really sinful, or do they merely think themselves morally superior to the men of Cranmer's day? One thing, at any rate, is certain: to play down the wickedness of sin is necessarily to devalue the wonder of the forgiveness of sins – a logical connection which those who belong to the Church's fundamentalist-chic wing should be made to understand.

The fact is that modern liturgies have simply gone the way the rest of the language has gone – vacillating, over-blown, euphemistic, weak. The hold on reality has slackened and we do not know where we are. Liturgies are what define our religious affections, our spirituality. So if these become euphemistic and unreal, then our psychological and spiritual life is bound to become degenerate, only neurotic. By contrast, the Book of Common Prayer is a true psychological-spiritual description of what it is to be a man. Aesthetic and literary quibbles about the quality of its language compared with that of the alternatives are only secondary issues. The language of the Prayer Book is better because it is truer. And if the issue of truth be held to have no significance for the solving of questions about what represents quality in literature, then we are on a very slippery slope indeed.

Psychological and spiritual validity is not the only issue: there is also the political question. The Prayer Book was hammered out of the painful conflicts of national independence and civil strife: King against Pope, Parliament against King, people against people. That it was a work of political genius is shown by the fact that the Settlement held. It was an astonishingly relaxed and liberal Settlement which peacefully accommodated the previously conflicting interests of Sovereign, Parliament and people – created a Commonwealth. It was no piece of finery, political old lace from an era of gentility but a powerfully reasoned political solution to problems that were always severe and often bloody. The oath of allegiance to a monarch without constitutional power is nothing but a profound affirmation of the oneness of the people beside which today's exclamations about 'democracy' seem sham. There were the Thirty-nine Articles but no more stringent religious tests. The people were in the cure of the clergy who, no doubt, were expected to make them faithful and devout; but extravagant enthusiasm, so called 'commitment', was never asked for, and if Englishmen received Holy Communion three times a year, including Easter Day, that would suffice.

In due course, various Acts of Parliament for the toleration of dissent were added to make the Anglican Settlement a most envied political solution throughout the world. And the essence of it was Commonwealth, loyalty, solidarity, the very practical application of the injunction to be members one of another. And it was founded, as all lasting settlements must be, not on abstract principles but on a communality of *interests*. So much in modern politics has got so far away from the importance of interests as to regard material objects, farms, lands, houses and money as filthy rags. This may sound very fine, idealistic, almost spiritual but, since men's minds are for most of the time occupied with material things, it is only a retreat into the tenuous world of vaguely connected ideas and abstractions. Politics must deal with the real world, that is with the organization and distribution of tangible particulars. Values are derived from objects, not the other way around.

Just as psychological and spiritual integrity must be founded upon what is an accurate description of the mind and the soul, so the nation must be created out of a true understanding of communality, Commonwealth. And these two foundations are connected. There is no possibility for the individual to achieve spiritual integrity in a neurotic society – no sanity in Babel; there is no chance that society can proceed peacefully when it does not consist of individuals who believe in and have interest in that society. There is much talk today of the need to create 'one nation' again, to shape a state which will attract the willing loyalty of all its members. The acrimoniousness of contemporary politics and 'sectional interests' and the bitterness of industrial and social conflicts – men were murdered in England in the 1980s for trying to go to work – make it more than ever desirable that we should recreate the Commonwealth. This cannot be done without the recreation of English culture; for religion, education and social and political life are cultural – that is, they demand some *form*. We cannot live by abstractions. As long ago as 1925, Eliot caught the way we were drifting:

> Shape without form, shade without colour,
> Paralysed force, gesture without motion.

And in *Four Quartets* he speaks of men 'distracted from distraction by distraction'. These are clear pictures of contemporary society, a society which has lost its hold on the language which gave it original impetus. All is individual, but individual sameness, strident but ephemeral, urgent but soon forgotten, expected to provide springs of moral action but at the same time only a matter of opinion. Social cohesion and personal morality must be constructed out of things more solid than the latest fashion in the mass-media and mere matters of opinion. We must rediscover the world of definite, tangible particulars. We must learn again to approach particular realities. This means the rediscovery of the language which most plainly and directly refers to reality. This is incarnation, Word made flesh, the language of God.

It is a language which signifies for everyone. The eight-

eenth-century atheistic philosopher David Hume knew
very well that true perception of the world depends upon a
kind of incarnation, the mind familiarizing itself with
actual particulars in the world. 'Nothing in the mind not
first in the senses.' Plain, non-euphemistic, true language is
one which is measured by the accuracy and definiteness
with which it refers to particular actualities. We must
attend to what is local and tangible and refuse to allow our
minds to wander vaguely over that tempting range of
possibilities which some call 'theories' and others call
'ideals'. Only among particular objects and particular
people can we have a life that is in any sense real: empiricism in this sense is not the enemy of spirituality but a
necessary condition for its existence. 'Man that is born of a
woman'; 'With this ring I thee wed'; 'A certain man went
down from Jerusalem to Jericho and fell among thieves':
these words are incarnation and they show that what is
spiritual is always local, particular and tangible. Why all
the frenzy for the giddy ethereality falsely called 'spirit' or
even 'the Holy Spirit' when the central doctrine of the faith
is incarnation?

I confess that I do not see much hope that there will be a
return to our cultural roots, a return to sense. We have
refined our confusion almost to infinity since Eliot gave us
that warning in the 1920s. Particular individuals can do
something, though, even if it will have to be in a very small
way. There are churches which still use the real books.
There is private prayer based on the language of those
books, and that language has the power to inspire and to
make holy. There is the responsibility to be relentlessly
critical of all that is barbarous. This is the prophetic task,
for to criticize means to pronounce judgement. We do not
pronounce on the basis of our own opinion, however, but
on the indubitability which the language of our cultural
tradition provides. There, in those books, are the standards for everything else and it will not do to claim that

they are indeed inspired and then to translate them into other words. There are no exact synonyms. There is no synonymity in alternative rhythms. We have seen what happens when the traditional words are altered: accurate psychology, ethical cohesiveness and spiritual integrity simply vanish. And this is not a matter of opinion; it is a matter of what has become our contemporary experience in every area of human life from Saturday morning television to the crematorium's obsequious obsequies. We must restore those words to common use. They are the words which mediate the world of reality. They are also the only words we have which mediate grace. Grace is not mediated by what is graceless.

But on the basis of *what* might such a restoration be effected? The old Settlement survived for so long because it had the support of the people who held power and authority: Parliament, the university, the Church. We have come so far from the days when Parliamentarians – in 1928 – voted hugely on the issue of the Revised Prayer Book, that now the contents of the Book of Common Prayer itself are as mysterious to many in the House of Commons as the writings of ancient Shinto or the Upanishads. Certainly, our representatives in Parliament no longer care about what happens to the Prayer Book – there were few who voted in the recent debate on the Prayer Book Protection Measure. This is very bad news, for it means that Members of Parliament themselves no longer comprehend the basis on which our communality, Commonwealth, rests. The university, or 'universities' as we must now say, worship at other altars altogether – headpieces filled with technology, computers, alien *theories* about the meaning of literature such as Deconstruction which tells us that 'texts' in fact mean nothing. Well, in Babel they mean just that. But in a world of shared sense things would be different: there would be shared meaning, a culture, communality. As for the Church, we have seen what it has done.

> O wretched generation of enlightened men,
> Betrayed in the mazes of your ingenuities
> Sold by the proceeds of your proper inventions . . .
> T. S. Eliot, *Choruses from 'The Rock'*

There may not be much hope but such as there is will have to be put in individual human beings making outcry against the prevailing barbarism. For the people who have inherited the power once held by the old authorities are those who depend for their continuance in power upon the very forces of chaos all around: the Controllers of television companies, advertising men and the like. Evidence? The American President gained office primarily because he was a well-known actor, a man from the world of 'media'; the ruling Conservative Party in England gives over its election campaigns to an advertising company. All is image without reality. Echo without Narcissus. How long before our politicians will not need to *exist* but only to *appear*? Before all the churches have closed down and been replaced by electronic worship via satellite television? Well, what an individual can do is never negligible – there was a time when there was only one prophet in Israel, but he managed to find seven thousand people who had not bowed the knee to Baal. It needs many individuals to recreate a culture. But how to recreate culture on what now mediates anticulture? How to express value on the universal medium of television which thrives by operating a method which is valueless? If traditionalists ever dwindle so low as to become a tiny but very rich sect, they might think of taking out 'commercials' on television for the King James Bible and the Prayer Book: then we shall know that the end is indeed nigh.

The task is, as ever, the conversion of the world. This means that the powerful and influential must be persuaded to support and defend what is of value. Unfortunately, in a society turned crass and illiterate, it is almost inevitable that one wins the argument but loses the decision. But, 'take no thought of the harvest, only of proper sowing.'

Besides reading Prayer Book and Bible we can also turn to the creative and recreative power of great art in our cultural tradition. These works, of Eliot and Lawrence, of Wyndham Lewis and Joyce, of C. H. Sisson and Samuel Beckett in our century – as well as of Shakespeare, Mozart, Samuel Johnson, George Eliot and Thomas Carlyle in theirs – are proof that the light is not finally extinguished. And we should add to what is, encouragingly, a long list, the critical works of Leavis, Wittgenstein and Ian Robinson whose *Survival of English* and *Prayers for the New Babel* are tracts for the times. But the continuation of a world of art and letters, no less than a world of morality and religion, requires a culture, a Commonwealth. To claim that this must be built out of a veritable incarnation of language such as we find in Bible and Prayer Book is not mere nostalgia, the attempt 'to summon the spectre of a rose, or follow an antique drum'. There simply is no other way in which Commonwealth can be recreated. Sisson, who has travelled further into the waste land than most men in our century, recently wrote: 'For my part, I should be delighted . . . if the politics as well as the language of the Prayer Book could be made the basis of any future revision: and this for the sake not of the past but of the future.'

We must relearn the language of our culture, for it is the Word made flesh, the language of God. Only the language of God can speak human truth in the new Babel.